THE YEARS
THUNDER BY

Nick Jaffe

Copyright © 2020 Nick Jaffe

All rights reserved

The characters and events portrayed in this book are fictitious. Any similarity to real persons, living or dead, is coincidental and not intended by the author.

No part of this book may be reproduced, or stored in a retrieval system, or transmitted in any form or by any means, electronic, mechanical, photocopying, recording, or otherwise, without express written permission of the publisher.

ISBN: 9798630787811

Cover design by: Nick Jaffe

Dedicated to my mum, who taught me self-discipline.

INDEX

Constellation	4
Route	5
Additional	6
- Prologue	7
- A beginning, a departure	14
- Arrival in Berlin	21
- A cabin in the sea	29
- The Search	38
- Dreams & Destinations	48
- Wheeling dealing & broke	57
- Auf wiedersehen Berlin	66
- Learning how to sail	75
- An English departure	85
- An impossible start	75
- Biscay & Beyond	109
- The kindness of strangers	119
- The Canary islands	130
- Closer to satellites than	145
land	158
- Caribbean landfall	171
- New York	192
- Overland U.S.A	192
- Into the Pacific	217
- Palmyra & Beyond	231
- Western Samoa	

- Tonga & the final leg   255
- Land   275
- Afterword   288
- Acknowledgement   292
- About the author   293

SV Constellation

1972 Contessa 26, built by Jeremy Rogers of Lymington, England.

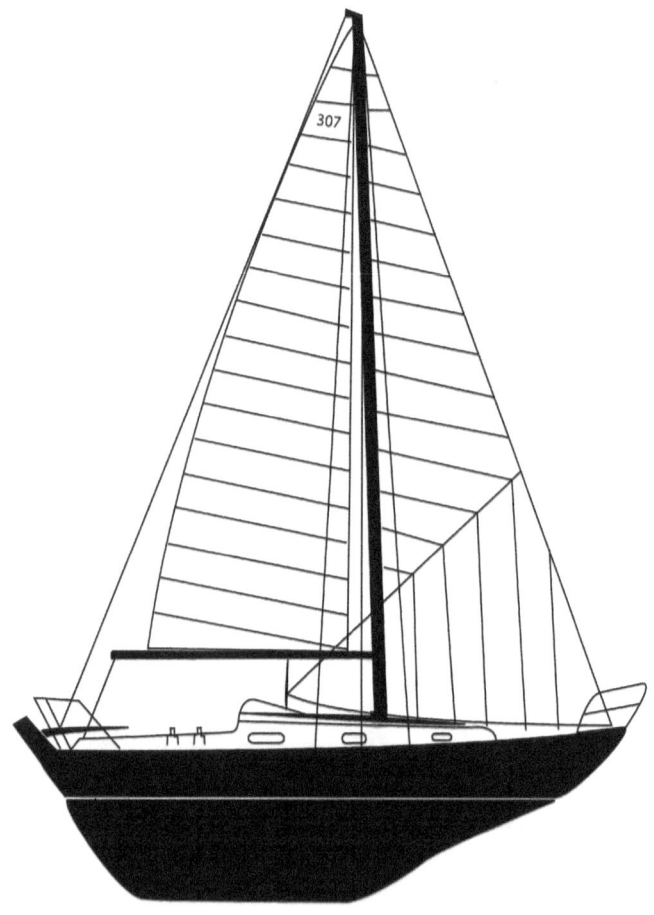

Route

Actual position markers captured by satellite phone

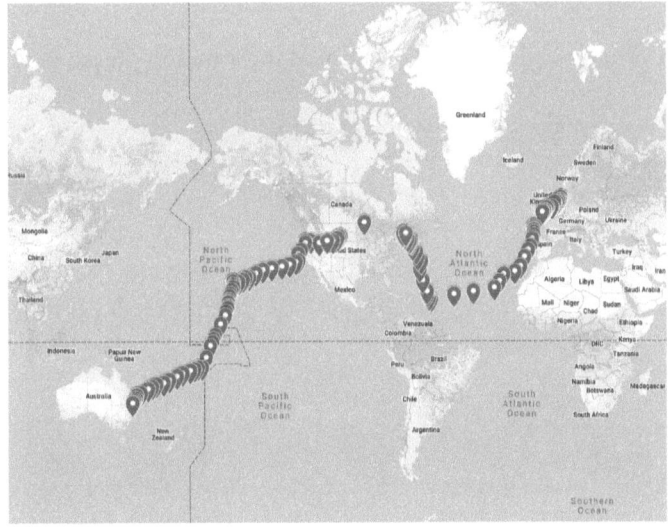

ADDITIONAL INFORMATION

For maps, photos and additional information please visit

www.theyearsthunderby.com

PROLOGUE

'Let everything happen to you: beauty and terror. Just keep going. No feeling is final.'
— Rainer Maria Rilke

The ocean is a tremendous expanse of power and beauty beyond all measurement - a *force majeure* of almost unknowable depths, covering seven tenths of our planet. Artists and thinkers during the 18th century tied these aspects of nature to the study of the sublime, and saw within this greatness, its counterpart: horror. Our love of the ocean comes not from its beauty alone, but from its ability to conjure a sense of both intense terror *and* awe. The non-dualistic and ever-changing qualities of the sea possess a scope seemingly beyond our grasp, and it is this intrigue which drives our love for its depths. For some, just the knowledge alone that such a place exists may compel them with great force to feel it all for themselves - at all costs, aboard all manner of vessel.

Constellation sailed unattended as I lay on the deck watching France go past from the English Channel. A seagull flew overhead and I dreamt of fish and chips on the nearby coast, people-watching from the park bench and the safety of its quiet harbour. Nearby, a cross-channel ferry steamed the gap, a group of high school girls giggled on the bow and a pod of boys on the stern threw candy wrappers into the ship's wake. I thought about the captain and wondered what he thought about small ships: how many had he nearly run down, rescued, or viewed with pity, or lay hove-to in an early autumnal gale? There was a lot to see out here - a veritable expressway of ships slow steaming in their respective shipping lanes, ploughing wakes in the sandy green water. Trawlers drew south, almost slatternly in contrast, into the Bay of Biscay to catch what little fish might be left. Tankers, too, headed for maybe Belgium, Amsterdam, Hamburg, Gothenburg, and the inner ports of the Baltic coastline. But not a single sailboat could be seen in any direction. No friendly white sails, no radio calls to say hello, no affectionate waves from the cockpit. I felt alone in the busiest seaway on earth, because I'm an idiot.

Constellation and I had been officially underway for five days. I'd avoided most of the North Sea by sailing on the inside of Holland and through the canal system. I exited Dutch waters at the extraordinary North Sea wall - a feat of human engineering which held back raging wintery gales from turning Holland into an underwater city and Germany's western borders into a newly formed waterfront. I'd crossed the English channel the night before to fill up on the less costly, tax free 'red diesel' in Dover. This was futile really: I could only carry about 20 litres in my small tanks, so the savings were negligible. In all honesty I think I just sailed across the Channel because I could, or because I was already longing for faint familiarity, something which felt a little like home.

Surprisingly the sun was out after a week of heavy rain. I felt melancholic, mostly from tiredness. The previous days had been spent at the helm, managing large Dutch canal locks and worrying about how late I was in the season to be attempting a passage south. It was already September and most boats heading for the Canary Islands to make their Atlantic crossings had left in June or July. I questioned my own reasons for leaving now - I always seemed to be in a rush. Sometimes my own ambition exhausted me. Or perhaps I was just growing tired of myself. I also felt that another season in port would most likely kill the voyage. I was terrified that the gusto, money and drive might wane and I questioned whether I could sustain the energy for another year. I kept telling myself *'the ball is finally rolling - let's get this thing done!'*.

This drive to completion made it all feel a bit like the voyage was just a box to tick some days, when it definitely wasn't supposed to be. I was trying to follow the path of salvation many had tread before, the path Thoreau had cemented in his many disciples, those of us burning with desire for solitude and wildness. But at times the machinations of daily life prevailed and these desires had to be reduced to a taxonomy of adventure. Is it important? How much will it cost? How much do I have? I had also, until now, underestimated my desire to keep moving.

There is an expression that sailors *'rot in port'*. It would take me some months, or perhaps even years to grasp what this truly meant. Sailors rot in port because they become swept up in busyness instead of the wind. Sailors know in their hearts that the sea is one of the few limitless and expansive landscapes we have left, and they understand the power these landscapes possess. Great horizons have the curious ability to support unimaginable dreams and mask distraction, allowing our gaze to meditatively focus on infinity: the impossible somehow becomes possible and dreams seem to become tangible. The space affords our dwindling ability for the laser-clear focus we are capable of but always distracted from. The fear, the distances and the constant dynamics of the environment remind us of how small we are in the universe and how little time we have; a sense which is so easily lost in the minutiae of daily life: in other words, *in port*. There is a profound sense of freedom, power and glory which surrounds the ocean, and for some of us this allure is enough to make us push off aboard small boats in order to not just dream it, but to feel it. Sometimes this magic is enough to make sailing off alone across two oceans seem not only completely possible, but absolutely necessary.

Yet, the reality was that I couldn't see any sublime

horizons at this stage. Various pieces of the European coastline and sheer terror kept interrupting my view. And, to be perfectly honest, I was ready to give up on this malarky and move into a monastery in France because attempting to sail across two oceans when you're a complete amateur is a terrible idea - and everyone around you will make sure you're reminded of it. I drafted an email to Plumb Village in France, a well known Buddhist monastery, pleading for them to take me in. Thankfully, they never replied.

So, I had a plan in place - it wasn't very well thought out, but it was a plan nonetheless. I'd picked the largest valve under the port bunk for the job and only a few minor logistical hurdles remained. I'd simply turn the valve handle, exposing the interior of my small boat named *Constellation*, to the exterior of the entire ocean. I'd then pull the release on my 23 year old liferaft, swiftly step up into its cosy rubbery interior, and wait. I'd nibble on some of the coconut energy bars inside the emergency kit and perhaps set a fishing hook over the side. This way, when I was rescued, I'd at least give off the impression that I was serious about survival. No one would ever be the wiser. The ocean is a great place to make things up.

Constellation was completely uninsured, so this plan wasn't about money, because no insurance company was insane enough to insure a 32 year old boat helmed by a complete novice in the open ocean. This was a plan to put an end to my tireless ambitions - to end this stupidity which would surely result in failure. I couldn't simply give up and fly home - the ending had to be dramatic. The story could never be '*Oh that Australian guy? He gave up.*' - I'd rather the dialogue be about my unfortunate collision with a Moroccan drug boat headed for Portsmouth and my consequent rescue by that cross-Channel ferry full of annoying kids. The story would turn into a love tale and segue into my meeting a beautiful teacher from Brittany on the bow of my rescue boat. I'd regale my story to a captive teenage audience on the bow of my rescue ship, and later tag along home to some quaint Breton villa to meet her parents over onion soup and wine the following week.

The truth is, I was afraid, under-experienced, overly dogged, broke and after just five measly days, I was done. The year of preparation, the dreams, the logistics: these required little risk, yet retained a hint of future excitement. Preparation is only a step up from armchair adventuring. You actually have to leave at some stage for the adventure to begin. It's why you meet a thousand old men with rolling tobacco in small tins holed up in marinas, clutching lists of lists of jobs requiring completion before departure onto warmer climes. I was swiftly learning that the adventure itself was perhaps not as exciting as the idea of it. Adventure, in reality, is a lot like writing this book - tedious, drawn out and lonely, with small but powerful hints of joy. On the upside, writing is considerably less dangerous.

While sailing, I thought about death a lot: what a ridiculous way to die, '*a waste of my own great life*' I thought. Such ego! How neurotic. I mean heroic. To die in a small boat in the Bay of Biscay, washed up on the shores of Basque country. William Turner's *The Shipwreck* (1805) depicts sailors and their boats flung against rocks, reduced to impotent miniatures against the ocean's strength and grandeur - was this to be me? I'm sure the Basque people had seen their fair share of vessels heaved onshore, pushed east by an incoming Atlantic gale, crew rotting like whales on the beach. Or perhaps I'd vanish mid-Atlantic, an anchor tied to my foot, mentally entwined in madness.

Quite frankly, I was afraid of myself, what others thought, what I'd started, and how this would really end. Perhaps in reality, I was afraid of saying I would do something I couldn't. In the Camus novel *The Stranger*, the character looks over the edge of a cliff and isn't scared of the height, but rather scared of his inner desire to jump. I was experiencing a similar kind of vertigo - I wasn't afraid of the hardship, the work, the risk. I was afraid of being truthful to myself. Truthful in the sense that perhaps I'd bitten off a lot more than I could chew.

So I kept going anyway.

A BEGINNING, A DEPARTURE

One calm Wednesday while still living in Melbourne, I turned up at the Sandringham yacht club to crew. I was picked up by the skipper after work and we discussed diesel sulphur contaminates (he worked for Shell Oil) as we crawled through peak hour traffic towards the sea.

Walking through the marina at Sandringham, we passed by the Sparkman & Stephens 34 *Lionheart*, formerly owned by Jesse Martin, holder of the world record for his solo unassisted non-stop circumnavigation of the globe at the age of 17. Laid up in a steel cradle, the poor old sloop looked unkempt and tired. I didn't know the story of *Lionheart* post-circumnavigation, nor did I ever imagine I would ever stumble across the vessel in real life, but it all seemed somewhat fortuitous. Later I would learn that every marina has one or more boats amongst the rubble which had powered big dreams. More often than not, such dreams had broken their owners, now vanished back to jobs and prior commitments, their houses and spirits mortgaged to the hilt.

One of the heartwarming things about sailing vessels, unlike cars or other material objects in our daily lives, is that each boat lives and breathes a story told by owners past and present, logged carefully inside books and folders hidden throughout the boat. Each vessel has its name, history, and birthplace. Drawers contain musty certificates and lined bits of paper full of maintenance notes covering filter types & engine hours, often cared for like a family photo album. I imagined *Lionheart* was no different.

I thought of old noodles from years ago, still stuck between bench tops, forever lodged as waves threw *Lionheart* sideways, tossing Jesse's dinner from his cold, shaking hands. I imagined him reading old manuals out of sheer boredom in the Southern Ocean, for things on the boat which no longer existed: old radar units, archaic depth-sounders, crystal controlled VHF radios and expired flares. I imagine he read everything, simply because he was tired of thinking his own thoughts.

At the race boat, my job was to crank a winch. I sat and I waited with my winch handle at the ready and my eyes on the skipper. The boat precariously backed out of its slip in a breeze, a job I would later find was often harder done than said, and off we motored past the breakwater. Still with my winch handle in hand, I patiently waited as we manoeuvred around into position, while other vessels dispersed around us to draw sail. With the boat pointing into the wind, things began to happen rapidly: bouncers bounced on halyards, the mainsail shot up the clanging metal mast and sheets tensioned. The skipper slowly motored to port, unwound the furler, whipped a sheet around my winch and yelled at me to crank. I didn't understand exactly how self-tailing winches worked and before long the foresail was over-tightened and the cursing began. The boat healed uncontrollably, we powered back up into the wind and someone else quickly loosened my sheet. Before I could understand what was happening, we were back on the wind, engine at idle, and everyone was happy again as if nothing had happened.

Before long the race gun was fired, and unlike a car race where cars screech off the start line, a yacht race starts as if everyone was starting an evening walk. We slowly lurched along, several other boats coming dangerously close before skirting behind us at the instruction of men in collared shirts on the bow, confirming and yelling distances off the bowsprit. We tacked, gybed and turned tightly around floating buoys in the bay. People yelled, I fumbled, the boat moved and the race continued until a finishing gun clapped the wind. The topping lift was loosened off, mainsail lowered, foresail furled, winch handles stowed, the engine revved and there we all sat - salted, cold, and perhaps a little seasick, motoring back to our slip.

For my first experience in a real sailboat, I guess things went as planned. All said, I didn't much enjoy the stress or commotion and the competitive nature of the evening didn't seem to excite me as much as it excited the rest of the crew. At this point, it's safe to say I had little interest in the finesse of sailing and most of my questions during the quiet periods of the race revolved around how far a boat of this pedigree could go, and for how long. I soon learned that the skipper had never actually sailed beyond the heads or out of the bay and into the ocean, even though the boat was more or less equipped to do so. I also learned that very few people actually venture off over the horizon, with their bilges full of tinned soup, to go exploring under sail. My only real interest in sailing was about the places one could go, and my suggestion that perhaps one weekend we could sail to nearby Flinders Island and catch crayfish was all but mocked.

Some weeks later, I lay huddled behind the spray dodger, poking my head around into utter darkness, a view interrupted by dozens of confusing lights from shore. The only lights we were actually interested in seeing glowed a faint green and red, marking the port entrance. It was my second race, this time of greater distance, which also included a return night passage. The wind had died some hours ago, killing the race for the entire fleet, and all that lay between us and the safety of being tied alongside a pontoon, was an invisible route in the darkness guided by a dimly lit compass.

For land lovers, our perspective and vision of forward travel is often augmented by a feeling of speed and progress. There is an understanding and sensibility of motion, time and place passing through a moving landscape. Yet, as I sat in the cockpit looking out, I was disoriented and slightly amazed that we could travel forward without having much of an idea of what lay directly in front, behind, or to our sides. I imagined this must be exactly what it feels like to pilot an aeroplane through a black night - you simply learn to trust that there is nothing immediately in front of you. We motored along in the darkness, not really able to talk above the thump of the diesel, each of us looking off into a black horizon - half keeping watch and half mesmerised in deep-thought, aided by the drone of the engine.

With each sail aboard crewed boats, I learned a handful of new jobs and better understood the dynamics of how a boat sailed, caught the wind, and needed to be held in a breeze. Yet, I also noticed that this style of learning wasn't compatible with my preferred method, which had always seen best results when I was left to my own devices. I felt uncomfortable being watched when I was trying to learn or do something new, always relishing time alone to tinker, make mistakes, read and study new things without any pressure. Even at school I couldn't bear being forced to do actual work in class, the teacher looking over my shoulder: it was impossible to think straight.

In the end, the competitive aspects of racing, my inability to be left alone on the boat to figure things out, and our lack of exploration beyond the buoyed course markers no longer held my attention. I stopped crewing, my studies at University winding up and my dreams making way for a new direction: Germany. My departure for Europe still lay six months ahead of me, so I worked as many hours as I could over summer, scraping a semblance of life savings together.

The summer before I left for Berlin, I went hiking at Wilson's Promontory. An hour or so out of Melbourne, the Promontory had long been one of my most loved places in the world. Before I left, I wanted to see again the long, isolated stretches of coast, granite mountain tops and thickly forested tracks. A day or so into the walk, overlooking Sealers Cove, I watched a sailing boat slowly motor into the small bay and set anchor. I'd not really considered that you could visit this beautiful part of Australia by boat, always connecting the stunning bays and campgrounds of the area purely with walk-in-walk-out access. The whole area looked martian, a fire having recently ravaged the landscape, trees defying death with prolific regrowth. Certain eucalypts require the chaos and heat of intense bushfire to strengthen and spread their seeds, a kind of inspirational reminder that nature often requires (and perhaps rewards) adversity over comfort. I often think we'd all flourish a great deal more if we took cues from the land and - metaphorically at least - burned our lives to the ground every once in a while.

A dishevelled man stepped onto the beach and fumbled with the oars of his tender. I was now standing on the pristine white sand and could see his yacht more clearly: a rust stained steel ketch, a red kayak hanging from its transom rails and green mouldy sail covers strewn across the boom. He dragged his tender above the high water mark and lit a cigarette. Barefoot in khaki shorts, a dirty white t-shirt covered in engine grease, a deep brown tan and a look of approachability. I put my pack down and walked over.

Sealers Cove was his last stop on a circumnavigation of Australia. His smile displayed deep sun-lines around his eyes, his demeanour was relaxed and friendly, a rolled cigarette held between his thumb and forefinger. We chatted briefly until I noticed my friends waiting at the end of the beach for me to catch up. I walked slowly along the beach looking at this unkempt but adventurous ketch. This was my first encounter with someone doing exactly what I had romantically envisioned as true sailing - a step out into the unknown, untethered. I imagined that the man I had bumped into was probably just a normal guy with a dream to go off adventuring in his rusty old boat. No crew, no commitments, no starting guns and no worries.

Retreating back to the walking path, we snaked our way up and over large rocks, climbing above the cove, looking down at the water to what I would never forget as my first inkling of what might be possible. I spent the rest of our hiking trip wondering about where I might sail to, completely forgetting the stifling heat, my heavy pack, my lack of financial resources or even my plans for Europe.

Returning home, I immediately jumped on the Internet and spent hours looking at boat listings. The dream rapidly diminished over the course of an hour when I realised that there was absolutely no chance on earth I could afford a boat. The ketch of Sealers Cove drifted out to sea and out of memory - for a time, at least.

ARRIVAL IN BERLIN

I arrived in Berlin during the month of May. It was bitterly cold, with patches of muddy snow persisting under the trees. The concrete surrounds blended into a grey horizon. The brightest object in every direction was the canary yellow M4 tram I was riding into Prenzlauer Berg. I hung tiredly from the rung with my bag, vaguely chatting with new friends I'd made on the plane. I wondered where north lay, struggling to get my bearings with the sun still in hibernation for winter.

Greifswalder Straße rolled by, revealing ground-level shops which sold mattresses and kebabs under repetitive four-storey residential buildings. The view from the sidewalk alternated between stretches of graffiti, the smell of rotisserie lamb and the tricolour flags of Germany hanging from balconies. I had, perhaps ignorantly, imagined Berlin to be a little more Parisian and a little less Stalinist.

Before leaving Melbourne, I'd organised a couch to sleep on through an online service linking travellers with city-natives. The idea of turning up in Berlin only to sleep in a hostel full of Australians run by a guy named Dave from Pittwater was not how I wanted to spend my first days in Europe. Alighting from the tram, I found a street corner Internet cafe to check for directions and any updates from my host:

Hi Nick,
Bad news, good news:
Bad news first:

I didn't indeed realize that I will be on a trade-fair in Basel, Switzerland for the greater part of the announced period of your stay. A typical double dating conflict induced by sloppy use of calendars, besides announcing it too late.

The good news:

I give my key to Philipp, a good friend and a neighbour of mine, so he will hand it over to you. You stay in my place until I return.

Sorry, I cannot really host you, not explain or show you anything, but giving you my keys is something I can offer you. And I hope I don't disappoint you with this offer.

-Jan.

Outside a block of grey flats, I searched along a grid of handwritten names beside bakelite brown buttons for

"Philipp". I pressed the most legible name starting with the letter 'P', the door unlocked and I began walking up the stairs into a distinct, cool, musty pocket of cold air emanating from the basement. Phillip was typically Berlin: Skinny, medium height, mid-30s, a delicate handshake, clothed in dark colours. We spoke briefly about the flight and he opened Jan's apartment, handing me the key without hesitation. I was effectively both a stranger to my new neighbour and a highly trusted guest of someone I'd only briefly written to on the Internet. This entire transaction seemed both generous and unattached, as if there was something less possessive and more humanist to Berlin, beyond my somewhat contrary first impressions.

The walls of Jan's apartment were an off-white stucco with unpolished dark wooden floors, dusty pot plants stood on small coffee tables, and unpretentious brown mid-century furniture sat beside lamps on three legged stools. There was nothing trendy or expensive about the interior. It emanated a sense of place rather than an intentional design-sense. In Melbourne, young digital agency directors would try to emulate this European minimalism in expensive inner-city suburbs, but this design seemed merely incidental.

Berlin had been the home of my great uncle Xaver Scharwenka and my great grandfather Philipp Scharwenka, both prominent musicians and artists during the turn of the 19th century. Their existence, along with the existence of my biological father from Stuttgart who died when I was 9 months old, were mostly just stories to me, unearthed in passing comments from my grandmother, mum, books and

Wikipedia. Xaver and Philipp had spent their lives crisscrossing Europe, performing and writing orchestral works. They socialised with Brahms' by the Baltic seashore and sailed past the Ambrose lightship into New York City with as much frequency as a financier aboard the Concorde in the 80's. These prolific brothers built teaching conservatories in Berlin and 5th Avenue, New York, held performances in the White House and carried pistols in their coat pockets. I recently found the Scharwenka family crest amongst a box of nails in the family shed. I sat quietly on a sawdust covered workbench, daydreaming about the distinctly polished and elegant blood I'd inherited, but could never match.

Franz is just a picture in my head. He leans over a Hasselblad 1000F with an 80mm Schneider lens and shares an exceptional likeness of appearance and physique to me. As I write, we are virtually the same age at the time of his death. When I look at images of him, we could be brothers, or he could be a contemporary doppelgänger living a parallel life on the second story of a Stuttgart apartment. His obituary reads:

"You will have tasted something of the depth of this man's thinking and probing... tasted something of his richness of his outlook, as well as something of the poverty of his hopes... And you surely will have sensed something of the tragedy of the world's impact on him... You may have sensed something of the struggles he had in wrestling through the many questions and deep issues of life..."

The poverty of my own hopes reaches an apex when I read this passage, not because I miss a person I cannot remember, but because I sense these exact words could be read out at my own early passing. If the exterior of my father has such tremendous similarity to my own appearance, I cannot help but imagine our brain chemistry must also hold similarities. I don't know if there is any scientific basis to any of this, but it makes sense to me - or perhaps it provides some sense of identity for me to cling to.

But he wasn't my father, after all - in truth, my dad is the man who raised me, a special man my mother would soon meet. Franz was a kind of spectral figure - an anachronism, a father figure from another time, perhaps in another world, another place. He looks out at me from a self-portrait, crossed arms, leaning over a Swedish camera, and I look back and imagine a melancholic twin who died in our infancy.

Soon after my arrival, I made new friends considerably faster than expected and began industriously figuring out my living situation. I viewed share houses adorned with black flags in nearby Kreuzberg. Rooms occupied by insanely friendly punks and apartments full of old computers helmed by dark eyed computer programmers wearing *Chaos Computer Club* t-shirts. I wandered down streets which appeared straight, but were topographically circular, becoming lost in an odd kind of *Bundesuburbia*, peppered with blocks of community gardens and demolished apartment blocks. Berlin was magical, dark, cold and loaded with mystery. By weeks-end I'd found my very own apartment just 200 meters from where I'd spent my first night.

Located above a small salami shop, I moved into my new *hinterhaus* (the often cheaper, darker apartments at the rear of a larger residential building) by inheriting the rent-controlled lease from a newly pregnant woman moving to the countryside. I was now living directly opposite the Hell's Angels, squeezed between the smell of sausages and the sounds of Harley Davidson's. Sundays occasionally brought neighbourly *Polizei* raids; blonde crew cuts, earpieces and guns knocking on the Angel's giant barn doors. The apartment was tiny and cold, a small balcony faced onto a dead garden without any view whatsoever, the bathroom featured a concrete shower basin painted in layers of blue gloss paint, presumably freshened by each new occupant. The saving grace of the bathroom was a transparent shower curtain with a map of the world - Iceland laying perfectly at head-height. Each room had a large coal heater constructed out of brown tiles over 2 meters tall, with a small recess and door on the front to warm your clothes, and a coal-pit in the base. It was quintessentially Berlin. It was perfect.

By late May, all I had was a sleeping bag and a piece of cardboard I'd found in the hallway to sleep on. Without coal for heating or any furniture, my first week was both freezing and the epitome of minimalism. Perhaps this scene sounds dismal, but, in actuality this started a period in my life which I've often considered as my happiest. I had the absolute bare essentials and no idea what tomorrow would bring. Summer was soon on its way and I began to watch the daily transformation of my surroundings, as the trees became green, and the people of Berlin warmed their wintery, gruff and sometimes unfriendly demeanour. I spent my first European spring simply walking.

After settling and scouring the streets for things to furnish my apartment with, I began searching for anyone who may have been distantly related. I knew I had some kind of family in Germany, somewhere, and I eventually found a woman named Marianne. I contacted her, attempting to explain my situation in German, translated from English on the Internet. I traveled to West Berlin for tea the following week to meet her. She was a distant cousin and I learned a host of new stories about my family, sifting through unseen photos stacked inside a dusty shoe box. Conversation was laborious, as we passed the thick German-to-English dictionary backwards and forwards across a small table covered in traditional German cakes. On another occasion we visited the Philharmonie in former East Berlin, where I heard stories of West Berliners catching the subway into East Berlin, through strict border patrol for a Saturday evening string performance. Everything we did, and everywhere we visited, seemed to possess a deep, dark history, with bullet scars still visible on building walls and inside memories.

While I had no set plans, there were some vagaries which were all swiftly forgotten. In every place I've ever visited, it has always astounded me how quickly and unconsciously environments influence ideas and futures. It's as if our surrounds contain a quiet, pervasive inertia and a large part of the puzzle in redirecting our own path isn't necessarily about working harder towards some lofty ambition, but rather about succeeding in finding a conducive outer environment to tease out our dormant actions.

Through new friends I met more friends, all within walking distance of where I lived. This too was a new experience - a sense of community, with friends on every corner. Punk musicians, doctors, and the odd Australian expat became my staple social circle. We'd go to concerts in Kreuzberg, have 'grill parties' in parks with soccer balls, play pingpong, drink 70 cent bottles of beer, watch football from TVs hanging out of windows on the footpath, visit art galleries, roam the circular streets of the city, and peruse the shelves of a nearby English bookstore.

I was unhindered for the first time in many years (or perhaps forever), able to drift in and out of situations and opportunities, at will, and without any preconceptions. The bolts holding me to the floor of my former life had rusted free and after all the years of school, work, relationships, and situational obligations, I began to recline into a far more comfortable chair of my own making. I was anonymous and free in a city full of gumption, with the weight of home lifting from my shoulders like a warm northerly breeze. I often pondered during walks, how familiarity, friends and routine are so very comforting - but they also tend to trap and conform us: it's hard to grow into someone new when you are constantly reminded of who you were. Coming to Berlin was an act of blind faith, it could not be boxed simply as finding myself, my family or my future - it was to allow new stimulus to unravel dormant ideas and dreams without hindrance.

A CABIN IN THE SEA

One morning in Berlin while casually browsing the Internet and with no particular goal in mind, I stumbled across a Swedish website for secondhand goods and real estate. Australians have a sickening obsession with real estate and as much as I wanted to separate myself from the property owning classes, my piquing curiosity about Swedish cabins felt involuntary. Ordering the page listings by price (least expensive), it was surprising to see a person could own a cabin in the woods for about the same amount of money as an old Toyota. This baffled me. I kept clicking around, and sure enough, in northern Sweden, a person of moderate means could own a cabin by a lake on seven acres of land. Primal strands of home-ownership DNA began to drive me into a property frenzy.

There is an undeniable thread of romanticism in living off the grid in our hyper-connected world. To sit quietly and deeply in the forest, to survive by wit, candlelight and grit. Right then and there, I decided I was going to

Sweden to live in a cabin through winter. I'd chop firewood, eat tinned corn beef, read dusty books by candlelight and write a memoir about my world in the dark wilds of northern Scandinavia. I'd be living a life crossed between Mawson, Jack London and Thoreau, penning my great work while curled up next to a Malamute through arctic nights. I might hunt a moose. Do moose even roam the snowy plains during winter? On second thought, do Moose even exist in Northern Europe? These were minor details at best.

Within a week I'd made contact with a seller in Stockholm and booked a flight to Denmark for 60 euro. I wrote to some strangers in Copenhagen through the Couchsurfing network to try to find a place to sleep and before long a self-confessed writer replied with a welcoming 'yes'. I ran down the musty stairs of my apartment, through the dead *hinterhof* garden, past the sausage shop and jumped back onto the M4 to the ring train. The budget airline was cramped. It would have been more comfortable for them to run overhead bars so we could all stand instead of pretending to sit.

I walked behind Copenhagen Central Train station en route to my couch for the evening, the backstreets striking me as unexpectedly gritty compared to otherwise ornamental and clean first impressions. I was greeted at a nice apartment by a thin man with large round glasses - he did look like a writer. The apartment was minimal, white, full of sunlight and touched with pieces of birch coloured furniture.

The following day I was up early after late night discussions on the usual topics of politics and life; the kind one has with intellectual strangers - gentle interrogations of values and feelings on the world shared by new acquaintances. He told me of his true love, a woman living in Africa. He'd even gone so far as naming himself the 'white African' in passing. According to his self-assessment, his philosophies and feelings on life resembled that of the African people. I glanced around his meticulous, Scandinavian apartment. Designer tumblers, an array of architecture books, polished floors. Who was I to judge?

Copenhagen was a transit-city for me, a logistical stopover on my travels into the far north. However, there was one thing I was particularly interested in seeing: Freetown Christiania. A self-proclaimed community covering close to 85 acres with up to 1000 inhabitants, located just near the Copenhagen city-centre. Exploring the community built on former military barracks, the space felt more inhabited by marijuana dealers than the fighting individualists I'd anticipated. Individualism has a disappointing tendency to fall apart in groups, perhaps diluted by competing desires for control. Or perhaps it is the misnomer that freedom is a close cousin to laziness, the truth being that freedom is actually built upon the foundation of discipline and hard work.

The bus wound down into Stockholm as an unfathomably deep purple sun rose along the starboard side of the bus. The light in these northern parts was like wearing a pair of Kodachrome glasses, the beautiful waterways, cobblestone streets and the buildings of *Gamla Stan* rose below. When I arrived at 4.30am, the city was bright like midday. The quiet calm beauty of a city before commerce.

Transfixed, I alighted to what seemed like the centre and walked along the water's edge, where I sat, my legs dangling over the side, waiting for a respectful time to call Gabriella about the cabin. Calling from a payphone at 8am, after fumbling with Swedish *krona*, Gabriella answered with disappointing news: the cabin had been sold in transit.

The answer to many of my woes was to walk. I walked through the streets of Stockholm pondering where to go and what to do. Uneven, steep, narrow, shadowed, beautifully signed, coloured. Would the cabin search still continue? Should I find an Internet cafe and continue the hunt? Was this a sign? Why not just keep going and see whether the far north of Sweden was even a place one would want to spend a winter? Perhaps the reality of the north was much like the reality of the Australian outback: mostly barren. Mostly inhospitable. Mostly a place for other people's nostalgia.

Thumbing through a roadmap found in a tourist information kiosk, the Swedish E6 highway was my route into the north. The far north. With new energy I walked briskly through the busiest centre of Stockholm, looking for a bookstore. Once found, I made a beeline for the photography section, focusing my interest on Swedish landscape photography. This seemed like the quickest way to hone-in on the most beautiful locations in Sweden: vistas of endless lakes, pencil pines, deep valleys, snow capped peaks, the northern lights, reindeer, lilac skies. Before long it was clear my dreams certainly lay north, as I turned and headed for the closest E6 exit ramp and stuck my thumb out.

Some hours later, I was still on the same exit ramp, with a sore arm and zero northerly latitude gained. At this point I was disappointed - I had some whimsical idea that of all the countries in the world, Sweden would be the most accommodating to hitchhikers. Unfortunately this was not the case, and before long I was at the central train station on a cheap sleeper cabin headed towards the arctic circle.

Exiting into bright sunlight at 4.30am, hundreds of miles from anywhere significant, I walked along the very vacant train platform, feeling hungry and tired. Sitting on a chair outside a small supermarket which eventually opened at 7.30am, I bought good, cheap, walking food: bread, cheese, bananas and water. I wasn't really sure where I was walking specifically, simply *north* on the compass rose was enough. I was now traveling north for a *feeling*. Perhaps I would seek endless sunlight, rather than any particular landfall, cabin, or grove. With my thumb out, I walked for hours across an expansive and desolate highway. Cars would drift by, swerving slightly to avoid getting too close and continue on their journeys.

After what seemed like an eternity and at a point where I was beginning to investigate a place in the forest I could safely sleep, a white Volkswagen stopped. A cheery Norwegian named Emil poked his head out of the drivers window to ask me where I was going. I told him I wanted to go somewhere beautiful and unique, beyond the arctic circle, a place where the sun never set. Being a Norwegian in Sweden, he naturally exclaimed the most beautiful places were over the border in

Norway, not Sweden. So I got in.

We drove over wet mountain passes, across ice, snow, and fog. Standing in front of a sign delineating 60 degrees north, Emil took my photo. The air was cold and the light was still brilliant at 10pm, as we traversed Blood Road in Saltdal, Nordland county. A place where bones from war prisoners lay decomposed amongst trees and lichen. The name of the road originated from a cross painted in human blood against a rock cutting, the blood falling from a prisoner shot along the route, the cross painted by his brother. I thought of my own brother. The seas of northwest Norway were geographically perfect for harbouring military ships and provisioning troops to further spread the German crusade. Through Blood Road we drove, a former camp of mass executions now littered in glistening trees, an orange sun, patches of snow and colourful native flowers.

Upon reaching a lake, Emil dropped me off to camp beside a fjord. The shore was covered in small rocks, a discarded floating red door, tree branches, and clusters of flotsam. The water was clear, cold, and still, with mountains stretching aggressively from sea to sky. At 2am, the sun lay low in the sky, yet remained bright; it was clear I'd reached the latitudes of an eternal summer sun.

With my internal clock completely turned upside down, I woke up the next day to an overheated bivouac at 9am and continued my trek along a road towards the Norwegian town of Bodø. The road narrowed on approach to a large mountain, an auto tunnel cut through its centre. Standing in awe by the road's edge wondering how I might safely walk through it, I was saved by an older couple who stopped and asked where I might be headed. After hours in the car with Emil, my mind was set on the Lofoten Islands. The Lofoten's were an archipelago of small islands, amongst the fjords and bitter waters of the Norwegian north sea. The couple agreed this was a worthy destination (each Norwegian I met made it their personal job to ensure I was getting my 'maximum Norway' experience) and off we drove through the tunnel.

The ferry left Bodø with plumes of diesel exhaust littering the stern as we headed away from the mainland into the fjords and islands of the Lofoten archipelago. We made short stops along the way at small villages to drop mail and locals into fishing towns, the region accessible only by water. Rickety wooden docks, colourful fishing cabins and expansive triangular fish drying racks covered in the white flesh of Atlantic Cod lay at every stopover. Each cod fish had been carefully splayed and hung out to dry for trade with Italy, a generational trading partner since the days of long boats. Houses lay perched against rocks, painted in vibrant variations of yellow and blue, dominated by the dark iron red of traditional organic paints, small piles of disused outboard engines and nets lay neat.

The disappointment of land ownership slowly washed away into our churning wake. In its place, old dreams of oceans and sails began to re-awaken, as I imagined what it might be like to sail amongst these tiny harbours aboard my own boat.

The ferry ploughed on, until our final destination of Svolvær appeared with its green mountainous backdrop, perched like a South Pacific island. I spent evenings in endless daylight, walking through town at midnight as if it was midday. Thick double black curtains were drawn across my south facing accommodation, mimicking a kind of darkness required by the more equatorially inclined sleeper.

The following day, I poked around military installations, sat upwind of the Cod racks and dreamt of sailboats. I dreamt of Wilson's Promontory and the rusty ketch, wooden boats, tar, and cold sea spray atop a military lookout, where soldiers once stood in anticipation of submarines rising from the deep. It was here, above the arctic circle, that the sea relentlessly beckoned.

A day later and with an increasing sense of urgency, I took a ferry to Narvik and boarded another train back to Stockholm. I'd surprised even myself at how far I'd ventured north, the return trip seemed to take forever, covering 19 hours of changing landscape. From Stockholm I caught a bus which included a ferry ride to Rostock across the Baltic. At lunch, the predominantly Romanian passengers all began eating chicken wings from tupperware containers. I watched on with hunger and curiosity.

On the final leg from the Baltic into Berlin, I considered perhaps how quickly I'd supplanted a cabin in the woods for a ship out at sea. Was I being fickle or are they one and the same? In comparative essence, a cabin or a boat were simply practical means to finding peace in a simpler, wilder world - a world of a romanticised past. To immerse oneself in elemental nature, a space which knows only one thing: the present. I must also admit, if it were not already plainly obvious, that I'm an unashamed romantic.

Without a job and with only $8000 in life-savings from my work in Australia, boat research in Berlin began the moment I walked in the door, two full days after leaving the Arctic Circle.

THE SEARCH

The search for a boat began quite simply with a question: who else had successfully done any kind of voyaging in small boats? What kind of boat did they have? I began at the beginning, with a history of small boat voyaging. I scoured the Internet, trawled eBay for secondhand books and perused the shelves of the local English bookstore in Prenzlauer Berg for anything and everything related to voyaging.

I soon discovered dozens of stories of madness, failure and heroism, each more incredible than the last. I came across Alain Bombard, the mad Frenchman who had crossed the Atlantic in a 15ft rubber inflatable boat in the 1950's, only drinking a small amount of seawater and eating fish he managed to harpoon or hook from the air-filled gunnels of his RIB. I ordered a copy of *South, The Endurance Expedition*, chronicling perhaps the greatest small boat voyage of all time - the *James Caird*. The *James Caird* was a lifeboat rescued from the ice-crushed vessel *Endurance* and had been just 22ft in length and carrying six men when it *voyaged* 800 miles from Elephant Island to South Georgia, a harrowing journey which led to the safe rescue of the entire *Endurance* crew.

From 1955-59, Canadian John Guzzwell successfully circumnavigated the globe in his tiny 20ft boat *Trekka*, which he built himself using only hand tools in a shed behind a fish & chip shop. His adventures also included the famous passage with the Smeetons through the Southern Ocean, told in one of my favourite sailing books *Once is Enough*. I later had the great privilege of meeting Guzzwell some years later in Berkeley, California. As if Guzzwell's boat wasn't small enough, Australian sailor Serge Testa took everything to the next level in the 1980's when he circumnavigated the globe in a 12ft boat in 500 days. His boat, named *Acrohc Australis* was so small, I often looked at pictures of it and wondered whether Testa could even lay down without bending his knees. Passion and desire for the open ocean knew no bounds.

After weeks of concentrated reading, I began to learn that exceptional ocean adventures actually had very little to do with money, and in many cases, skill. The underlying thread amongst everything I was reading was quite simply a story of pure, unadulterated tenacity, grit and intensity. Every small boat voyage I came across was driven by some kind of insane dream; to set off and experience something exceptional, regardless of perceived barriers, financial or otherwise. I had been previously hung-up on looking within the standard marina-culture of Australia and Europe, visually and morally drowned in the spectacle of all those boats, neatly lined up along the pontoons and slips. However, it began to become quite clear that what I was personally seeking wasn't to be found anywhere near these places. I was seeking something which was conjured up in backyards, won at betting tables, stolen, or bought for $500 off a lien-dock in Sausalito. The kind of boat and the kind of person I was seeking expansion from, was found deep in the crevices of the sailing world, outside the realm of magazines, gear, twilight racing, yacht club drinks and all the trappings of extremely expensive hobbies and possessions. I felt like this weird desire I couldn't really contain or even explain was beginning to find its home. Hopefully, even its people.

The Internet is an amazing place, it allows even those with the most obscure interests to find others who share the same things. You could be living in a tiny rural town with an immense interest in literature, only to be entirely surrounded by those interested in football - where do you find friendship? How do you feel less alone? How do you grow? The Internet is a special place for those who simply don't fit in, can't fit in, or refuse to fit in. I'd searched high and low, reading Shackleton and other sailing classics on my search, but these journeys had all happened in the past. I wondered: was anyone doing anything *today* from which I could garner inspiration? And so my search for contemporaries began.

Long before my encounters with the Ketch of Sealers

Cove, or in fact any sailing at all, I became enamoured with a woman who's name I was never able to rediscover, who lived on a catamaran somewhere in San Francisco bay. She was a graphic designer and her story was profiled in a copy of Wired in the 1990s, a magazine I used to save up for and buy whenever I could from the local news stand. My dad still remembered this story well into my 30s as being the true instigator for my interest in voyaging. As such, I spent days trying to find out who this woman was. In the end, I never found her (perhaps she was a figment of my imagination? Or maybe it wasn't *Wired*, but another magazine?), however I did run across someone of similar age, named *Moxie Marlinspike*, who lived in the Bay Area of greater San Francisco. Or, perhaps he lived in a squat, a shed, a rolling train, a decrepit boat at anchor, or anything in between. It was difficult to tell whether Moxie was a series of stories or in fact an actual person. We seemed to share a number of key interests (within technology and now perhaps within voyaging) and I reached out to him having come across an online journal of his photos. I don't have a copy of the email I sent him, however I have his reply:

Hey Nick, it's really nice to hear that you read my stories and liked them. It's also nice to know that you're thinking about the same things and dealing with some of the same issues. I have to admit, though, that it's a little strange whenever I hear that someone thinks I've got it figured out. =) I can assure you that the stories are just the highlights, and that I'm just as lost as anyone else. I sometimes wonder if the people that I'm inspired by feel the same way.

I can only assume from his reply, that I had gushed in some way about him having life figured out! For some reason, I still had this idea that everyone else had it all sorted out and I was the only one left on earth fumbling through the chaos of time. Moxie's photos were full of images of freight train hopping, completely unseaworthy small boats in the Caribbean and punk-parties.

Moxie had created an online mailing list called *Blue Anarchy*, where I discovered a tiny niche of low-budget sailors with big dreams. I wouldn't identify myself as an anarchist per se, however some aspects of the political philosophy, including a strong stance on freedom and autonomy did ring true to my own sensibilities. Amongst the ideological discussions, the mailing list was mildly interesting, although perhaps full of outspoken ideas on voyaging rather than a whole lot of *actual* voyaging. Talking about sailing and making plans to go sailing are perhaps one of history's greatest subjects of non-action.

My search for young sailors achieving great things on small boats continued, as Aron Meder began his journey through the Mediterranean aboard his 19ft ship *Carina*. With excitement, I wrote to Aron with my own ideas and to wish him luck - to which he replied a few weeks later:

Dear Nick,

Thank you for your email and good wishes:)
I hope we will meet somewhere (maybe in the oceans...)

My age is 26... so you are younger than me with 1 year! :))
(Unfortunately, I can not read emails very often.)
When will you start your trip?
What is your route plan?

Best regards,
Aron

I trawled Aron's website using Google translator (the site was in his native Hungarian), to glean as much information as I could on his trip, boat setup and equipment. His equipment was basic to say the least, and the boat seemed poorly chosen in terms of seaworthiness in the open-ocean. As it turned out, it was: *Carina* was built in the landlocked country of Switzerland, presumably for weekend lake sailing. Yet, the takeaway from all this was the joy in discovering someone of the same age, who was *actually sailing right now* around the world in a cheap boat which was not even designed to touch saltwater. As Aron sailed, my resolve grew even firmer.

Soon after my discovery of Aron, I discovered a young german named Johannes Erdmann, who at the age of 21 had recently sailed a boat designed for Baltic coastal sailing across the Atlantic, solo. The boat was now for sale in Florida for about the same amount of money I had saved in the bank. I thought to myself, 'well, if his boat can cross the Atlantic, I'm sure it can go to a whole lot of other places too' - I quickly wrote Johannes an email expressing my interest. His reply was friendly and he seemed genuinely interested to hear of my ideas about sailing, but unfortunately (or rather, fortunately in the end), his boat had sold. So began an invaluable and long dialogue of emails, which resulted in a kind of mentorship over the following year.

My final discovery was a Norwegian couple, sailing a beautiful 26ft boat named BIKA. It's one thing to sail a 26 foot boat alone, but another to sail one as a couple: if you do the sums, that's just 13 ft each, almost as mad as Serge Testa! Their boat, a Jeremy Rogers Contessa 26 struck me as being beautifully proportioned with clean lines and a sense of sturdiness. The boat had a classical look to it, with low freeboard, a long full keel and simple transom hung tiller steering. The more I read and understood about voyaging, the more I learned it wasn't about money, size or even gear. In most cases, it was actually about robustness and simplicity (perhaps a philosophy worth considering beyond just voyaging). BIKA was a British built Contessa 26, a boat which also turned out to be the choice of solo circumnavigator Tania Aebi and other young sailors who had successfully completed significant voyages. Johannes had also suggested the Contessa 26 and in my research it came up again and again as a worthy choice of boat.

My list of small boats which had proven themselves in the open ocean was getting narrower, as I honed in on my requirements and geographic location (there was no point looking at designs primarily found in South Africa, for example). They were all small, generally tough and had a history of being helmed on long voyages by predominantly young people in their twenties, or men nearing retirement age who had thrown the towel in and followed their dreams. There is definitely a personality and age pattern in low budget small boat sailing, since you really have to be at a point in your life where external burdens are at their lowest. Mortgages, families, lovers, expensive lifestyles and possessions are all virtually incompatible with small boat voyaging. Ultimately, it's a dangerous and all-consuming endeavour which requires some hard choices, which is where most people get tripped up, fast-forwarding their imaginations to anchorages in the Caribbean before doing the hard work. The boat, technical details of voyaging and all of the periphery technicalities are not show-stoppers - it's almost always the transition from a burdened life to an unburdened one which is the hardest.

The notion that solo-sailing is a selfish endeavour has come up in conversation on more than one occasion. The idea has always confused me as I feel the vast majority of us live wholly for ourselves, yet we will rarely admit it or take the time to understand our choices and circumstances as being predominantly self-serving. The aforementioned incompatible lifestyles (families, mortgages, love etc) are no less selfish, all ultimately serving our fears, comforts and vices - simply in a more common and recognisable way. There is a significant economic (both personal and financial) penalty dished out by society for not adhering to the rules, and one will experience significant judgement and scorn on the journey because of it. The world more commonly rewards traditional labours; the shovelling of dirt and the building of houses over artists, solo sailors and vagabonds. One must prepare for a lonely and difficult path to live as an outlier.

Slowly my list of possible sailing boats was whittled down:

S&S 32
Island Packet 27
Orion 27
Sabre 28
Vancouver 27
Catalina 27
Contessa 26
Achilles 24
Cal 24

I researched each boat in detail, considering where they were most often found, their average price, general availability and their ocean voyaging history. In the end it was quite simple: I felt the Catalina was too lightweight, the Achilles and Cal were too small and all the others were too expensive. I lusted dreamily over the S&S 32 and the Island Packet 27, both beautiful boats of excellent pedigree, but well beyond my financial abilities. The singular remaining choice in the group was the Contessa 26, which I was already leaning towards. The Contessa was still more than I thought I could afford (but then again, they all were, I had virtually no savings left), yet it had a proven track record and were readily available in nearby England, where they had been manufactured since the late 1960s. In the end, everything, both practically and emotionally, pointed towards the Contessa. These beautiful little boats had a long ocean-going history, were available in England and weren't astronomically more than I thought I could manage financially. I decided it was good to push my financial goals within reason, the idea being it would motivate me, but not to the point where it might demoralise or destroy me. With a final decision made on the Contessa 26, I was mentally freed up to figure out how exactly I was going to afford one. So the hustle began.

DREAMS & DESTINATIONS

I was so enamoured with the landscape of Norway that throughout the entire journey home from the Arctic to Berlin I dreamt about sailing along the Norwegian coast, my small boat entering and exiting the dramatic passageways of the fjords under full sail. When I'd finally made it back to Berlin, I read about katabatic winds and Williwaw's - the plummeting winds which drain from high elevations, causing sailors great distress while transiting fjords. These winds were most notoriously experienced by early adventurers exploring the fjords of South America, as they searched inside the Beagle Channel for a quicker route into the Pacific. I imagined a dark winter above the Arctic circle after a summer of sailing north, my boat hauled out of the water, working short days in a local fishery and sleeping long nights in the seemingly everlasting darkness. The romanticism I had attached to the whole concept seemed to know no bounds: the places an imagination can go once it's hooked on the open sea is almost unfathomable, as though my mind had opened up to another reality where physical and mental borders had ceased to exist. Thor Heyerdahl said with more clarity: "Borders? I have never seen one. But I have heard they exist in the minds of some people."

As I dreamed, researched and connected with other sailors for guidance, a curious thing began to happen. Buying a boat and sailing off didn't actually seem to be an entirely impossible dream anymore. Like any complex new subject, from the outside it seems magical and beyond comprehension for a while, yet as you spend more time on it, the puzzle starts to unravel. The mind, given enough motivation and work on a particular subject or idea, has a beautiful capacity to shift gears into a state where abstract dreams start to break down into a series of tasks, resulting in a new reality. The stages of a big idea or dream often follow a common path: the first stage is excitement at the possibility. The second stage is the dread of details: *"Is this possible, how is it possible, what about this or that"*. The third stage is often a loss of the dream; a drowning in a spiral of minutiae. The fourth stage is the make-or-break stage: is the dream quashed or is the dream verbalised; has the conversion phase into reality begun? The fifth stage is living in the new reality: one's life must begin to revolve around the dream, transition into the dream, create the dream. Sacrifices are made, focus becomes singular. The change within your community and your network begins to take place as they understand your new direction and your momentum builds. It's easy to dream and fail without ramifications alone in the night, and another thing entirely to have some external accountability; to be vulnerable. Once the final stage into vulnerability is complete, the dream has morphed into a reality. Certainly, it could fall apart and you're at the risk of embarrassment, loss and failure, however that is another set of phases - at its core though, you are well on your way.

I began to wonder: if I could sail in my head along the fjords of Norway, could I sail somewhere further? The boat I'd decided on was certainly capable, but was I? In this new reality where I can sail anywhere in the world (in my head, at least), I'd ask myself whether I could sail further ashore. The Caribbean? If I'm going to sail to the Caribbean, perhaps I could sail across the South Pacific and into French Polynesia? Before long the idea was expanding exponentially: could I sail all the way home to Australia? The fjords of Norway were beautiful and challenging, however, on a return walk from the supermarket, I had somehow decided the ultimate challenge would be to sail all the way back to Australia from Europe. To sail home. To discover what was between here and there. And in this brief and unlikely moment while walking along Greifswalder Strasse, the idea which I would obsess over for the next three and a half years was born. The idea only required a few small details to be ironed out over the coming months and years: namely a boat, how to sail, navigate, finance the idea, etc... (big ideas first, details later!).

My life in Berlin was isolating yet wonderful. I spent the majority of my time either walking outdoors and thinking, spending time with new friends in local parks, or at home in my tiny flat alone, reading and researching. The pressure of daily life was at an all time minimum, the cost of living in Berlin was manageable with the resources I had, and while I still retained a long distance relationship with my girlfriend in Australia, the daily pressure of maintaining a traditional relationship was gone. I looked for work briefly, but even as a German citizen, my job opportunities were limited because of the language barrier. I had citizenship through my biological father, though unfortunately the gift of the Germanic language was not subject to such inheritance.

In my search for work to cover my rent, I spent a night working as a human vodka dispenser. Lugging a backpack full of vodka with a hand pump, I'd follow young American tourists from club to club, shooting vodka into their mouths with a small hose, much like I was killing weeds along the side of the road. I barely made it through the first night and never returned. I kept looking high and low for work, trawling English notice boards and Internet job search engines. Every day that went by without money coming in, was a day funded by my meagre savings. As I honed in on Contessa 26's throughout Europe, I began to realise that financially I had a quarter of what I actually needed and zero job prospects.

Between job searches, I read sailing books and built a website to chronicle this new journey. I knew I couldn't very well announce such an idea to the world without something firm to back it all up, having no significant experience, no history in sailing and little capital. How could I build a website and boldly pronounce I was going to sail single-handed across two oceans? I couldn't. I built the website as if I was going to announce the idea, diarising the journey from the beginning with utmost honesty. The website remained invisible to the public, using it as a sketchbook to chronicle my ups and downs, my job woes, my ideas, goals, routes and even books I was reading, as if I was talking to a real audience. The website was a great motivator, giving me a taste of the pressure I would feel once I had put the idea out into the world. I knew the idea was mad, knowing full-well once I'd made it public that I would have to be able to hold up to criticism. I also knew deep down that maybe no one would care. I'm sure many young men have boldly proclaimed they were going to sail across the high seas, only to be quickly dismissed by everyone around them, soon giving up and going back to work. Part of my secrecy in the beginning of the project had a lot to do with protecting the fragility one has at the beginning of a big idea: if you announce it too early, negative feedback from friends and peers can easily set you back. Conscious of this, I knew I had to keep the dream tightly on the inside, while feverishly grinding on the exterior details. Mulling this over on another of my long walks through the suburbs of Berlin, I decided I would announce the idea as soon as I'd secured a boat.

It was clear work in Berlin was not going to materialise. The kinds of jobs which may have been available were careers. I didn't want a career. I'd left school at 17 to pursue a career, working out fairly quickly what it really meant: comfort and stability. The goals I was interested in were the polar opposite of comfort and stability, and as such I'd need a job which was flexible and reasonably well paid. I learned quickly that while Berlin was an amazing place to live, it was not an amazing place for work. The unemployment rate in the former East was in excess of 25%, making the job market competitive and low paying, not to mention an added layer of difficulty in grappling with the language barrier. I did know Berlin was good for me mentally and emotionally, as it was conducive to working on big ideas, was affordable to live and I enjoyed the small network of friends I'd built up. However, it was clear I needed a new strategy.

I began looking to England for work, searching job websites for anything I might be able to do while remaining in Berlin. The pickings were slim, yet I came across an unusual looking privately posted ad for a programming job, in a programming language I had a modicum of familiarity with. The pay wasn't great and neither was the office location, situated in the suburbs of London, which meant it wasn't attracting the kind of interest it may have normally. I wrote the job poster an email with my CV, saying I could do the job for a discounted rate of £12/hour (extremely low at the time, given the job market and cost of living in the UK) on the provision that I could remain in Berlin and work remotely. Out of nowhere I got a call for the job from a man named Oliver, who spoke with a strong northern

English accent. After a brief and to the point conversation, it was clear Oliver was absolutely desperate to find someone. We agreed to some basic terms, one of them being that there was enough work for me to work as many hours as I wanted. With no commitments and no distraction, I knew I could easily work 12 hours a day, maybe more if I had to. I said yes straight away, but quickly realised after I'd hung up that I had a small problem: I didn't actually have a computer capable of working in the environment he required. I waited an hour and sheepishly called Oliver back asking if he could forward pay me a week's wages so I could buy a computer to work on. He laughed and said he'd drive one over. "Drive one over? To Berlin? From London?"

Less than 48 hours later, Oliver turned up from London with an IBM desktop PC in the trunk. In an extremely bizarre and short meeting, he left his girlfriend double parked in a black Opel hatchback out front, as we hauled the equipment up the stairs. He glanced around my apartment with a look of horror: I had a trestle table made with an old door, a mattress on the floor (I'd upgraded from the cardboard mattress) and a pile of sailing books. Oliver knew that to get the skills I had back in London would cost at least three times what I was asking, not to mention all the hassle of hiring locally on the books. The deal was a good one for both of us. Even though Oliver knew I was roughing it, it felt like he also knew I was extremely motivated, even if he didn't know the exact reason for it. As soon as he'd left, I plugged in and started work on the project, a software system for booking & routing taxis through London long before the days of Uber. The software was complex and cobbled together, the codebase was difficult to understand, full of scrappy work and hacks. It took me a full week just to understand what was going on before I was able to make any progress on the project. Many hours went unbilled because while I had some experience in the programming language it was written in, I was by no means an expert and felt guilty at the prospect of charging for my time to learn on the job. Unfortunately it would turn out my honesty was not reciprocated.

As I worked day and night alone in my apartment, I'd take breaks to peruse online sailing forums, walk around the block and update my website with any tidbits of news on my project. The days were long and lonely, my eyes red and my back sore from countless hours at my trestle table. In my breaks, I'd found a Contessa 26 in England and made some low-ball offers which were all courteously declined. Days turned into weeks, as my time began to flitter away implementing optimal driver routing code into Oliver's application. After two weeks of intense work, I began to realise my idea of maintaining 12 hour days, 6 days a week was untenable. I also began to notice Oliver was holding me back, as he slowly retracted his offer of working as many hours as I wanted, creating excuses and roadblocks to slow me down. I guess he imagined I wasn't going to take him seriously, grinding out features and bugs in the codebase seemingly around the clock. By the third week I was down to thirty hours.

By week four I had found a Contessa 26 in the south of England for £7500, while sitting on £2000 of savings and no additional buffer. Oliver had still not paid me for my work, but I naively trusted him. The boat was tired looking, the hull suffering from osmosis - essentially, waterlogged fibreglass. Everyone will tell you that "a boat with osmosis has never sunk" which is probably true, but the more one reads about it, the less one lusts after a waterlogged boat. They can of course be repaired, the process is simple but expensive: you plane the hull back and sit the boat undercover with infrared heat lamps directed at the damp fibreglass. After a week or two, the boat is dried out, re-fared with gelcoat and the hull is back to being shipshape. The boat was beautiful, as all Contessa's are, but the osmosis bothered me. However, it was also the osmosis that made the boat cheap, making it a difficult situation. I wasn't a purist looking for the perfect boat, I was really just looking for a boat that could affordably and safely get the job done. The vessel wasn't of enormous importance at the end of the day, I kept reminding myself of the title of Lance Armstrong's book "It's not about the bike". I was lucky in a sense, because I was completely utilitarian about the whole thing. It really wasn't about the boat at all, it was about the process, the adventure and finding out about oneself and about life. The joy of boats would develop later.

WHEELING DEALING & BROKE

I wrote a long email to the broker selling the osmosis-plagued Contessa 26, weaving a long story about my intention to visit remote islands, perform singlehanded crossings of two oceans, cross the Bay of Biscay and other fanciful oceanic challenges. When I re-read email today, I can't help but think he must have thought how tremendously naive I was. Yet, perhaps it was such an unusual communique in comparison to his usual brokering, he had a brief moment to dream and think back to his own youthful sailing imagination of vanishing across the horizon. Or, on the other hand, perhaps it was the sure-to-fail payment scheme I pitched: I'd developed a risky idea to ask for seller finance on the vessel, which served two purposes: firstly, it would allow me to open up the project to the public and perhaps attract some interest (because I had an actual boat, not just an idea), and two, it would put me in a position where I was hyper motivated. In my mind, having 'skin in the game' pushed me into a risky place where I had virtually no other option other than to succeed. The details of the deal were as follows: I offered £6500 for the boat, with a £2000 deposit due immediately (literally all the money I had in the world), after which I would owe monthly repayments of £1000 for another 4.5 months until the boat was paid for. In addition, I would pay for any marina fees during the payment period. If at any point I missed a payment, the broker could walk away with my full deposit and any money I'd put down. When I reconsider this idea today, I definitely know the broker wasn't reminiscing about his youth. I can only assume he believed I wouldn't be able to maintain the payment scheme, hoping the boat would be up for sale again in a few short months, having made £2000 or more from this curious sales diversion.

As I was preparing the money which would seal the deal, I did a few last-ditch searches around Europe for boats, and noticed a new Contessa 26 named *'Constellation'* enter the market. *Constellation* wasn't suffering from osmosis, had a near-new engine and even an old life raft, for a similar asking price. I immediately re-drafted the email I'd sent to the first broker including full details on my ludicrous payment plan, and sent it off with my offer. The broker soon replied and said he didn't think it was something the owners would be interested in, so I begged him to just run it past them and waited impatiently while stalling the other Contessa purchase.

Four days went past before I heard an answer, just moments before I was about to revert to the previous purchase: the answer was yes. As it turned out, the owners were romantics and loved the idea of their boat sailing the south seas. I'm sure they also loved my flimsy payment scheme, but I was nonetheless full of excitement and nerves. I wired all the money I had the same day, leaving nothing left for food or rent. The next day I silently pushed my website live and told no one.

Having worked a full month by this stage, the time had come for me to send my first invoice to Oliver. I emailed it off and heard nothing for two days. Two days became three, then four days, and before long a full week vanished without communication. I began to become concerned. The software system I was working on was a live platform, with taxis actively using the software to book and route drivers. Oliver still hadn't responded to my emails after two weeks. During this time I also didn't have any work to continue with. Rapidly, the first month's boat payment started to creep up. With no money, I had no food and no ability to pay the rent. The rent could probably be stretched, but food? Not really.

Berlin has a recycling scheme whereby you can collect bottles from the street and put them into a vending machine at many major supermarkets. With no food, no money, a fraction of a boat and a boss who had gone completely awol without paying me, I began walking the streets late at night, collecting plastic bottles. I raided bins, jumped fences and carried everything in large garbage bags. Within a few hours I'd more than filled a shopping trolley, which I took to a nearby supermarket. I cashed all my bottles in one at a time, the machine vending a docket to the value of the bottles I'd collected. It was enough to buy food for the next couple of days. I couldn't afford luxuries, but it was enough for simple essentials like canned lentils and pasta to tide me over.

The next morning after a late night on the streets collecting bottles, I'd still heard nothing from Oliver. He wasn't responding to calls and my patience was running thin. Feeling powerless and angry at the hole I'd dug myself, I became anxious bordering on manic. By the third week, I decided if I was going to be ignored (which I knew I was, I could see other parts of the system were active under his maintenance), I'd yield the only power I had and change all the system passwords. I locked the entire platform down but still kept it running, emailing Oliver with what I'd done: pay me what I'm owed and I'll surrender the passwords. It was blackmail. He replied within minutes and he was understandably furious. By day's end I'd received a letter from a lawyer (which I look at now and see was clearly falsified) threatening to capture me at the U.K border next time I visited for cyber blackmail. Nervously, I called his bluff and remained steadfast: pay me the hours I've worked and everything goes back to normal. Within 48 hours he paid and I surrendered the passwords.

With enough money to pay my rent, the first instalment paid on *Constellation* and food on the table, I was back at square-one with a very seriously burned bridge behind me. The whole situation made me feel sick.

A week later Oliver called me. The number came up on my mobile phone and I could barely stomach the idea of answering it. Astonishingly, and after an awkward 'Oliver?', he apologised for what had happened. I also apologised - I felt terrible about the whole situation, but I literally had no money left (yes, this was bad planning on my behalf), no food on the shelves and the real possibility of losing the boat I'd financed on strenuous terms. I explained to him what was going on, the boat, my dream to sail to Australia, the owner financing and my need to work. Interestingly, he started to understand my motivation. Oliver really needed me to continue work on the system and I obviously really needed the work. I told him I'd think about it for the day, eventually deciding if *he* took the burden of risk by paying me 30 hours a week in advance, I would continue working. He agreed, asking me to fly to London to work with him in his office so we could go over some curly issues that were better solved in person. This was perhaps his way of ensuring I didn't just take the money and change all the passwords again (understandable).

The following week I flew to London, with the idea to actually go and see *Constellation* for the first time as well as get some work done. I'd spoken to the broker and arranged with the owners to be allowed to sleep on *Constellation* for a few nights. I flew into Heathrow, trekked down to Gatwick and nervously met Oliver, considering the real possibility that perhaps he was actually flying me over to break my legs - I had a sense about him that leg breaking behaviour wasn't entirely beyond his capabilities. Oliver had said he would organise a hotel for me near his rented office, which sounded good. In a last minute change of plans, he then mentioned that it would be easier to stay with a friend who was also nearby. I wasn't too sure what was going on, but I slowly began to realise Oliver was actually more broke than I was. He couldn't actually afford to put me in a hotel, and was putting me up at a friend's sharehouse who had a room free. I was dropped off at a stranger's house without much of an introduction and sat down in the kitchen, bewildered. I walked down the street for Indian takeaway, returned, and went to bed, the sound of strangers walking around, TV's and the smell of cigarette smoke. I lay in my bed dreaming about *Constellation*, perplexed and a little mad at myself, at how good I was at getting into curious situations.

The next morning, Oliver picked me up and we had a traditional English breakfast of blood pudding, hash potatoes and tea at a cheap diner in a grey English town. His rented office across the road, was a tiny room in a large stack of temporary offices you could rent by the hour. There was nothing in the office but a picture of some daffodils on the desk and two computers. We drank instant coffee and sat under fluorescent lights for 5 days straight, my misery reaching a new peak as I seriously wondered if even the high seas were worth this. I ended up only staying at the share house for the first night, before Oliver decided I should stay at his house with his girlfriend and her son, my situation taking a new dip when I ended up sleeping on the bottom bunk of the stepsons bunk-bed. Oliver would take me out each night with his girlfriend to a local pub and buy pints of beer. I wasn't much of a drinker but I felt my situation was so dire I could easily polish off three pints if someone else was paying. Hell, I even took up smoking menthol cigarettes, standing around the pub talking to strangers about absolutely nothing interesting at all, wondering if my situation could deteriorate any further. At one point I couldn't work out if I was misreading the dynamic or not - whether a pint or two more might land me an exceptionally awkward invitation into their bed for the night. With luck, no such invitation arose.

After two weeks, I eventually made it to *Constellation*. Oliver had paid me as promised, and I'd managed to make my first payment without a hitch. I met the broker, took a bus into town and returned with snacks, tea light candles and a £15 sleeping bag. *Constellation* was musty and damp, the bilge was full of water for reasons I couldn't understand (she lay on a hardstand, nowhere near the water!), but otherwise she was more or less what I had expected. Which, to be fair, wasn't a lot considering I'd never owned a boat before in my life. I spent the night snacking on chips, reading old manuals and studying the small diesel inboard engine.

Constellation lay at a brokerage in Bursledon, a quaint, classically British village alongside the River Hamble, near Southampton, perhaps best known for wooden warship building in the 1700's. I would later walk past remnants of one of Henry VIII's fleet further up the Hamble, the frame of the ship poking out of the river like the carcass of a long-drowned animal. The Hamble, which lay metres from the cradle supporting *Constellation*, ran out into The Solent, perhaps one of the world's greatest yachting centres, meaning I had rather accidentally put myself in the epicentre of British sailing. This wasn't intentional - I really had no idea about English boating at that point, however it would end up being one of the most important parts of my rapid education about sailing and the water.

I spent another few days on *Constellation* before I had to return to Berlin, soaking in as much as I could from anyone who would talk to me. I was normally a shy person, not being one to talk to strangers unless it was absolutely necessary. However, I felt myself opening up. The people around the marina were eager to talk, particularly when I mentioned I had my own boat. Mostly I spoke to old men, their hands covered in paint and varnish, often found walking around with tools in their hands, perhaps intrigued by someone relatively young with their own boat in the yard. I tried to keep a lid on my ambitions because I knew I was naive and ill prepared to discuss them, but I let slip my tentative plans in one conversation. It wasn't long before everyone knew what my dream was and I was garnering a whole range of unsolicited advice and sideways glances. I had no tools nor money, so I couldn't set about doing any work on the boat (I also only technically owned just under half of it by now), so I mostly explored the area, talking and walking the docks, trying to soak it all in. Everything was entirely new to me, the language of sailing, the culture, the expressions. I would spend hours in the nearby chandlery reading books I couldn't afford, studying and learning.

AUF WIEDERSEHEN BERLIN

My then girlfriend of seven years, soon arrived in Berlin. Over the previous nine months our relationship had been barely held together through phone calls and emails. She knew about my dreams, yet they were rarely spoken about at such a distance. I imagine in a sense perhaps she felt (or hoped) the sailing trip would never really happen, which I suppose was a real possibility... Why rock the boat when you don't even know if the boat is going to exist? So much had been happening over the last nine months, there was a definite sense when I finally picked her up at the airport that a lot of water had gone under the bridge. We had been together since I was 19 years old and this had been the longest time we'd been apart. I had a friend who had recently broken up with a long-term girlfriend which was unexpected, his reasoning being *"when I climb a mountain and look across the valley, I don't want my first thought to be that I miss my girlfriend!"*. I thought this was an obscure answer, but in a way it kind of made sense, as in I could understand the metaphor at least. I started to imagine myself out sailing along across the Atlantic, amongst the stars, the phosphorescence, the wildness, the storms, the magic of it all, pining for my girlfriend back home. I wondered if this would ruin the experience. I wondered if I really had to do it *completely alone* in every sense of the word. Or was it just selfishness talking? I'd never been alone in my 20's before and I started to wonder what it might feel like, to just feel completely free without any responsibilities to anyone or anything. There are so many conflicting emotions when you think about projects of this kind, it's hard to work out what's real, what's imagined and what's just an excuse.

As it would turn out, I did end up completely alone. One afternoon in nearby Volkspark Friedrichshain, a park I would often go walking in to think about sailing, we sat on a large rock together and discussed how things were going to work. The last few weeks had been tentative as she began to see my dream was perhaps more than just an idea, it seemed to dominate everything. We sat side-by-side, our legs dangling over the edge like kids on a park bench. I tried to reassure her I could meet her in different places around the world, although I would have to do the actual passage making on my own, as I had committed to doing the trip solo. I don't remember today whether she asked to come or not, but I think back to that day on the rock as one of my few regrets. If I knew then what I know now, I would have taken her with me in an instant. We would have voyaged around the world like crazy vagabonds. I read back over our emails and conversations from that time with a heavy heart, realising I'm sure, like many before me, that they had lost someone special in search of something new.

My work with Oliver had dried up and the boat was virtually paid for, but that was just the beginning really. Owning a boat is one thing, having it ready to sail somewhere over the horizon is something else entirely. I bought a cheap suit on the way to the Schönefeld Airport for an interview in London I had the next day, for a high-paying technical job at Condé Nast. I arrived in London and stayed with old friends, waking up early to iron the fold marks out of my crumpled shirt and head off to my interview. In the heart of London I found the building, boarded the elevator and stood amongst five beautiful women all towering above me with long legs. They were models for one of the publications, and I began to wonder what kind of life I was potentially about to embark upon. The elevator stopped and the five women alighted into a large modern office. I kept going higher, eventually reaching the 'technical department', where not a single model could be found. I went into a small interview room and was promptly grilled for an hour. I was 26, applying for a job as a lead developer at one of the world's largest publishing houses, which had me punching well above my weight. I left the interview knowing I hadn't left an impression. I took the next train to Southampton unsure of what the future held. I wasn't holding my breath for the role, but I did know that if I did get it, within a few short months I could have made enough money to fund virtually the entire trip, earning £300/day - almost triple what Oliver was paying.

Back on *Constellation*, I pumped the bilge dry again, still perplexed as to why the bilge was filling up with water when on land. It was the tail-end of winter by this stage, with the odd nice day showing itself through the grey English sky. Mostly it was absolutely freezing. Without a heater onboard as I couldn't afford the electricity, I'd light the cabin up with handfuls of tea-light candles for both light and warmth, waking throughout the night covered in condensation. I was happy though, really happy. All my work had paid off and here I was on my boat. There was no looking back. I wondered around the boatyard the next day pondering what I was going to do about money - a never-ending theme. I'd applied for a few more technical jobs, but in all honesty I just wanted to be with *Constellation*, not wanting to spend another hour in front of a computer whilst dreaming about being somewhere else. Walking up the hill to the supermarket, there was a chalkboard out front *The Crows Nest*, a local pub, seeking staff. I'd never worked in hospitality before, having been charmed with software related jobs since my mid-teens. I applied and soon got a call back to get started. The pub was only a 15 minute walk from the boat, the pay was £7/hour and I could work part time, mostly the late afternoon to closing shift.

My life started to get into a rhythm, working late nights at the *The Crows Nest*, making new friends behind the bar who all supported my sailing ambitions, asking me everyday what I'd been working on or reading. I spent my days working on *Constellation*, figuring out whose advice to take around the boatyard and who's advice to politely ignore. Every Thursday I was paid for my pub job, usually around £180-200/week. Every cent of it went directly into the boat. I'd eat untouched leftovers from plates returning from the pub restaurant, or the chef would sneak me chips and the odd bowl of curry when he could. I had no debt, the boat finally paid off, and each week, I just needed a few non-boating essentials to keep going (food when I wasn't working, etc). On the odd occasion patrons at the bar would help me get parts or materials for my boat. I never really asked where they came from, having a sense they probably came from somewhere that wasn't a place where goods were exchanged for money... One regular in particular was a risk assessor at a major bank who seemed to know everyone and everything. His job was to work with hard men along the docks of Portsmouth who ran fishing boats, working out how to help them stay afloat on their lines of credit. I couldn't say for sure, but I suspect these fishermen were the source of some of the gear which landed on *Constellation's* decks. When it was time for *Constellation* to be launched I didn't have any fenders (rubber inflatable tubes to protect the boat along the dock). When I awoke on the morning of the launch, a local turned up with a nice set of six fenders as a present. Later I was to find out he had assembled the set by walking the docks late at night, stealing just one fender off much more expensive boats to make a set! Help was coming from the most extraordinary and unexpected places.

In the boatyard, I met a couple named James & Emma who were not too much older than me. They could often be heard arguing with each other like absolute banshees from across the water. They lived in the back of an old Transit van with a motorbike somehow crammed in there with them, doing odd-jobs on boats around the marina. I ended up becoming great friends with these two, often having dinner with them or drinks when we both had a bit of spare money. James was an amazing sailor with a wealth of knowledge and experience, who was also eager to help me. I could tell he knew I didn't really know what was going on, but I also knew he could recognise my drive. He knew I was eager, willing and hardworking and could tell good advice from bad advice, even if I didn't know the specifics of why a particular piece of advice wasn't right. Perhaps he also felt a sense of responsibility, knowing I would sail off whether I was capable or not. James became invaluable to me in refitting *Constellation*, always listening to my ideas and endless questions. Emma was lovely, always encouraging, always ready to help and constantly trying to keep James in check. James was constantly coughing and wheezing from being a dire asthmatic who smoked two packs of cigarettes a day and drank far too much at every opportunity.

When I was in Berlin, I'd met another Australian at a bar. I wasn't really one to even go to bars, however that year the soccer world cup was in Germany and I was dragged along to a match. It was there that I met filmmaker & editor, Jack Rath. We hit it off as friends and met up the following week. I began talking about my trip, how I'd bought a boat sight unseen on the Internet; how I was going to sail back to Australia without any previous experience - the usual story I told people that either thought it was an awesome sounding idea or that perhaps I was mentally unstable. Thankfully, Jack thought the idea was interesting. He was always searching around for an interesting story to document and he decided to bring his camera around to my house the following week, just to ask some questions and see how it all looked on camera. In the end, he came back to me and decided he would just keep filming and see where the idea went. Jack and I would continue to be great friends as he followed me and the trip closely as the months went by.

After months of work, *Constellation* was nearly ready to launch. Jack flew over from Berlin to film the event, helping me late into the night finishing final jobs. I had completely rebuilt the rudder from scratch, cleaned, painted and made numerous hull repairs, among many other tasks. There are dozens of disparate systems on a boat, even small ones. To service and manage every single system to be fit for ocean voyaging on such an old boat could take forever, so ultimately it was about choosing the most important systems to get right. From thinking about it and working on the boat over the last several months, it was clear to me that at the end of the day, it was really just three key things: Keep water out, the rudder intact and the mast upright. Everything else was of course important too, but I didn't have an unlimited budget or unlimited time, so these key factors were what I concentrated on. I replaced all the thru-hulls, completely blocking unnecessary ones, such as the head (toilet) outlets and old engine cooling outlets. The standing rigging was less than ten years old and showed no signs of fatigue. I replaced turnbuckles, re-seized them correctly and replaced sheets & halyards. The mainsail (as was the rest of the sail wardrobe), was at least 20 or more years old. I really needed a whole new set of sails, so began my first foray into asking for financial assistance. I emailed a friend who ran a company back in Australia, whom I once worked for. I explained the situation, how far I'd come and what I needed. Graciously and surprisingly, he funded a brand new mainsail, *Constellation* receiving her first sponsorship sticker along the hull.

Constellation lay in her cradle, re-painted a bright apple red. The paint was bought for a song out of the back of a truck, with only two colour options: blue or red. I remembered BIKA, the Norwegian Contessa 26 with her red hull, and decided to emulate it for good luck. With her rebuilt rudder, polished topsides, new mainsail and freshly applied sponsorship sticker, it really looked like we were going on an expedition. As I progressed with everything, I continued to update my website with every detail, with every sponsorship attempt and every modification. Over time I garnered more and more support, with people who lived nearby often traveling down to the boatyard to help or offer support or advice after reading my website.

As *Constellation* was lowered into the water, I began to

see her for the first time afloat. Out of the water, *Constellation* didn't actually appear to be that small, perhaps because of her full keel. However, in the water, she began to look absolutely tiny, seemingly half the boat disappearing underwater like an iceberg. I felt a tiny pang of fear run through my stomach as new friends gathered to watch the launch and celebrate. I sighed with relief after jumping onboard and confirming no water was gushing in from anywhere, instructing the crane operator to begin removing the straps. *Constellation* then floated completely on her own for the first time in many years. She was a beautiful boat no doubt, but after so much work and stress, the true enormity of what I was trying to do began to hit me. I'd been working so hard, there was barely a moment to really even grasp the reality of what I was embarking upon, and that I'd actually have to start sailing pretty soon. The weather was closing in and I was already very late in the sailing season to even be contemplating my trip south to the Canary Islands, where I would begin my voyage across the Atlantic ocean.

LEARNING HOW TO SAIL

Constellation was towed from the crane to her berth alongside a pontoon with a boat to her bow and one to her stern, parallel parked with barely any room to move. I hadn't yet completely figured out the engine but I bought a new battery, serviced it and gave it a try. Amazingly, the little single-cylinder diesel came alive, sputtering after not being started for years. I was chomping at the bit to motor around the river, though I was also terrified. I'd never actually driven a boat out of a slip before, nor even sailed a boat with a tiller! I needed a quiet day with no one around watching - there is nothing worse than being the spectacle of a marina, as you reverse your boat out and into a neighbouring boat, dragging your bow down her sparkling gelcoat. I made a plan for the coming Monday morning, begging Emma to come with me and help. She took the day off and we fired up the diesel, untied the lines and tried to sneak her out of the slip with as little fuss as possible. Unfortunately, I had not calculated for the running tide, the River Hamble constantly moving, causing me to completely miscalculate my exit. *Constellation* banged all the boats near her on the way out, Emma trying her best to fend us off. While my tidal timing was well off, I had at least timed things well enough so that no one was watching! Eventually we were free in the river, motoring down the Hamble under a blue sky. Sweating with nervousness, Emma stood on the bow with excitement as we motored up and down the river. The feeling was amazing, *Constellation* was underway and we were actually going somewhere! After an hour of navigating up and down the river, it was eventually time to get *Constellation* back into her slip, which was a hundred times more nerve-wracking than exiting it. I approached my slot a number of times, learning the intricacies of how *Constellation* manoeuvred, learning to go as slow as possible while still keeping underway. Miraculously, and with Emma's help, we tied up with success.

With *Constellation's* new mainsail fitted, we were ready to really go sailing. I decided to wait for another quiet day in the boatyard, as this time I would attempt heading out entirely on my own - my first solo sail. I pre-prepared all the halyards, sheets and sails on the dock to make things as easy as possible. Without any kind of autopilot, I needed things to be easy, knowing full-well the panic that can take hold when things inevitably start to go wrong. I had the tides correctly timed as we motored out of the slip, cleanly exiting without a hitch. Motoring as slowly as possible, I ran up to the mast to try hauling up the mainsail, leaving

Constellation motoring and unattended, constantly running back to set the course straight so as not to hit one of the hundreds of boats lining the river on moorings. Backwards and forwards I ran, hellishly trying to raise the sails for the first time, quietly thinking to myself how impossible this was going to be in an actual sea as opposed to a quiet, flat river. I was stressed but happy to be completely on my own without the added stress of having someone around to either tell me what to do or make me feel self-conscious. I knew I learned things more efficiently on my own, free to make mistakes without judgement, to learn at my own slow pace. Eventually the mainsail was raised, I cleaned up the sheets and decided to leave the foresail alone, having been challenged enough raising just the single sail for the day. I had a paper chart on my lap as I navigated down the river, deciding I would head out into Southampton waters rather than stay on the river.

Happily motoring along with the mainsail raised, I promptly drove *Constellation* directly onto a sandbar. Not just any sandbar, but an extremely well marked, famous sandbar which everyone knew about, except for me. Thankfully the tide was at its lowest, as I sat there watching boats motoring past me. Ferries, yachts and motorboats all waved in amusement at my misfortune. Embarrassed and angry at myself, the coastguard soon came alongside and asked if I was ok. I said I was, just waiting for a bit more tide to back off the bar and continue into the Solent. Amused, they left me alone to wait, where I sat for an hour before *Constellation*'s long keel could be worked out of the sand. My nerves were shot and I decided I'd had enough for the day, turning around and motoring back to my slip. At the very least, I'd successfully managed to raise the sail, exit and return to my slip and learn about what it feels like to be grounded. There is a common expression which states that if a sailor claims to never have ground his boat, he's either lying or has never set foot on the decks of a boat in his life! That's what James told me that night as we drank beer, played pool and smoked cigarettes, feeling better already. That night, after we'd both had enough to drink, we decided we should sail to France in the morning for no other reason than to buy a bottle of wine.

Cherbourg on the French coast was virtually a direct line from Southampton, a short detour around the Isle of Wight, just across the English Channel. The next morning we woke up feeling horrible, but the forecast to attempt a passage to France actually looked pretty reasonable. After pestering James to get out of bed and eat something so we could leave, we eventually headed off down the river by late morning. Completely unprepared with just some cereal onboard, a few litres of water, a French coastal chart I borrowed from someone down on B dock, and a handheld GPS I borrowed from someone on C dock. We set out, and with James knowing the Solent by heart, we promptly navigated correctly around the sandbar. There were boats *everywhere*. Ferries, work boats, yachts, motorboats, fishing boats. It was a veritable nightmare of sea traffic. James kept course, having me hold the tiller as he calmly pulled up the mainsail, sheeted off the foresail and de-powered the engine. For the first time, *Constellation* was under pure sail. James pushed *Constellation's* rail underwater, and flying along at the theoretical maximum speed we could travel (an actual speed scientifically governed by the hydrodynamics of the boats underside) with all of our sail up. I was terrified something would most certainly break, but James seemed undeterred. Perhaps he was still drunk. Yes, I decided he definitely was still tipsy as we flew on a starboard tack towards Cowes on the Isle of White, water gushing into the cockpit and seeping through the portholes (yet another job to complete). James handed me the tiller and reached into his pockets, only to realise he had forgotten his wallet. We couldn't sail to France without any form of ID, so James gybed the boat and we started sailing back from whence we came. He called Emma, who met us at the closest marina we could pull into. Back on the Hamble with his passport, we stopped for a brief second and headed back into the Solent, the sun beginning to set as *Constellation* ploughed into the English Channel under a red sky.

James chain-smoked into the night as we kept a close eye on the heavy traffic through the English Channel. I felt seasick but incredibly happy to be out of sight of land. *Constellation* was performing beautifully, although our progress was slow and choppy as the predicted winds swung onto the nose, making forward progress wet and slow. Being unprepared, we weren't carrying adequate wet weather gear, and by midnight we were both soaked to the bone. I tried to get some sleep, *Constellation* pounding head-on into sharp waves, water pouring in through port fixtures and hidden seams in the deck, as I curled up in a wet bunk, water seeping onto my legs. I took careful note of where all the water was entering, which wasn't hard because water was essentially entering from *everywhere*. I rolled James cigarettes in the moderate dryness of the cabin as he took large amounts of spray off the deck. By midnight, James called the trip off, saying the conditions were becoming too ridiculous to continue. I suspected the alcohol was wearing off! I had no real baseline for sailing, so I couldn't tell whether this was normal or more difficult than usual. We turned around and things became calm, sailing on a more gentle tack, moving with the waves instead of pushing against them. I took over and James went below for a nap, as I huddled into the corner of the cockpit, nervously sailing by the dimly lit compass as we headed towards Portsmouth. One hour on, one hour off, we took turns at helming and resting, but never sleeping, everything was simply too wet. We eventually made it into Portsmouth, tying up alongside Alex Thomson's enormous race yacht *Hugo Boss*. *Constellation* looked like a matchbox toy against the stealth-like chines of Thomson's multi-million dollar sea-weapon. Without sleep, we drank coffee and ordered large fried breakfasts at a local diner, both pleased to be warm and off my godforsaken boat.

Sailing back to the boatyard, we tied up and slept for the rest of the day. I woke in the late afternoon and tidied *Constellation* up, my entire life was inside the boat and had been thrown every which way. Old charts and knickknacks were to be found in unusual places, bits of food from who-knows-where were lodged in the now full bilges. After setting things back in order, I started taking notes on the evening's events. What had I learned? What needed to be fixed? In all its simplicity, what I had learned was that one needs to prepare with great consideration before voyaging, so as to lower the burden while at sea. The importance of this is because everything at sea is at least ten times harder to do. I started to understand where the meticulous nature and culture of keeping one's yacht 'bristol' (the term for a beautiful, perfectly maintained boat) came from. It may have become a sign of prosperity and showmanship, but its roots actually come from ensuring oneself and the yacht is fully prepared. The nature of this attention to detail is twofold: if one keeps every inch of their boat in excellent, well-maintained order, they both have prepared themselves for the difficult nature of being at sea and also ensured their own understanding of every minute detail and system, for which there are many. A boat is almost a self-contained ecosystem, to the point of almost living and breathing, perhaps because it is actually in a constant state of decay and flex from the harsh environment it lives in. Boats are so often referred to with names and treated as if they were human, something I often think is because a boat is quite visibly and constantly dying, always requiring maintenance, attention, patience and work.

I continued to work on *Constellation*, pulling port fixtures, deck fittings and anything else which wasn't absolutely necessary. Sleeping at night on my narrow bunk, the smell of wet caulking slowly drying in every crevice , the interior of the boat crammed full of borrowed tools, tubes of silicone and chaos. I sailed whenever I could muster the energy to pack everything up and set off, making short overnight trips to anchorages around the Isle of Wight, admiring the beauty of waking up afloat, drinking coffee from the cockpit in peace and silence. *Constellation* was like a little self-contained spaceship; we had everything we needed onboard. Anchoring felt like a short trip into space, the anchor chain rolled out across the seabed. Land and the rest of the world felt somehow otherworldly, as if we were part of a secret new territory. There was an 'otherness' to everything, as if I was in an orbit of distant observation in my own little world, fully self-contained and free. When I'd sail back to the boatyard and tie *Constellation* up, the feeling instantly evaporated.

As the major jobs on *Constellation* began to dry up, there was a feeling in my bones that the time was nearing for me to really get underway. I was still unprepared in many ways, both mentally and also in terms of overall readiness. However, I was particularly unprepared when it came to my finances. Every bit of money I'd earned working had gone straight into *Constellation*, with virtually nothing left over. I fearfully looked at the calendar, the season for sailing to latitudes further south was rapidly dwindling. In addition to the more calculable barriers (money, knowledge, preparation, etc), there was a much larger mental barrier: my crossing of the infamous Bay of Biscay.

The crossing was unavoidable, in the sense that I

couldn't just spend a few months casually sailing along the coast of western Europe, 'getting my bearings'... I literally had to depart from England and jump off the deep end. The Bay of Biscay was notoriously difficult for sailors, a place renowned for harsh Atlantic weather which could push sailing boats deep into the bay, creating untold shipwrecks and an uncountable loss of hands. Any mention to others of sailing to Australia would always ignite a warning and dramatic tale about the Bay of Biscay. The passage itself wasn't particularly long, calculating it could be done in 3-4 days, however it would be my first multi-night voyage alone, and it was all I could think about every night. I distracted myself from it all and tried to focus on my finances and preparation. There was nothing to be done about it; no magical way to avoid this significant leg of the voyage. No way to ease-in.

Through long days and nights I would ruminate on all of the barriers in front of me: The Bay of Biscay, my lack of money, lack of experience and all the rest ... the list seemed endless. Days were rapidly ticking by and work at the pub making minimum wage was barely enough to live on. There was enough each week to buy a few small things for *Constellation* and eat something meagre, but it simply wasn't enough to get ahead: I'd dug myself into a survival rut. *Constellation* also still didn't have one of the most critical pieces of gear required: self-steering. A solo sailor cannot sail without a way of steering the boat when sleeping, navigating and working the boat, which is always underway.

The most simple and reliable self-steering for a small boat like *Constellation* was called a windvane. Essentially, the windvane helps steer the boat on a constant relative course to the prevailing winds, utilising only the wind and forward movement of the boat to generate steering force. The concept is difficult to explain, but in reality it's just a finely balanced vane which is constantly tweaking the boat's steering relative to the wind in order to keep it on course. This piece of equipment was rare to find secondhand and relatively specific for a boat of *Constellation's* size. I couldn't find anything on the secondhand market, with a new vane running into the thousands of Euros. I began to feel defeated, hyper focusing on this one piece of gear, a pivotal part of the setup and virtually as important as a mast and sails when it came to solo sailing.

This roadblock, a lurking sense that I was underskilled, my total lack of savings and the rapidly closing seasonal weather window pushed me into a decision that I would need to delay the entire trip by a year. The truth was, I needed to sail somewhere where I could live on my boat, close to a major city and work for the next 12 months. I was utterly disappointed and defeated. A lot of momentum was required to keep thinking this was all possible. I needed small runs on the board, positive forward progress.

AN ENGLISH DEPARTURE

With a new but disappointing plan in place, I began to make ready for my departure from England. I felt deep in my heart that I'd pushed so hard to get this far, that perhaps if I delayed the trip for a year I wouldn't be able to maintain the energy. I was so afraid of failing at what I'd set out to do. In addition, my voyage had become quite public in a sense, too, with many people encouraging me on my way, reading my blog and offering a helping hand. It was silly, but I felt that I was going to let others down as well as myself, or open myself up for criticism, yet I really couldn't see any other avenue.

My new plan was to live on my boat through winter in a major waterside city, to save on rent and maximise savings, in either Amsterdam or Hamburg. I already knew that it was going to be a brutal existence, particularly through winter. However, both of these cities were water cities where I thought I might have a chance of finding more lucrative work while still being able to save money, living aboard. Working at the pub only provided me with a survivable income, and I needed an income which provided all the necessities for the boat as well as enough savings to get me at least a few degrees further south.

By this point I *still* hadn't sailed anywhere significant on my own. I'd sailed a lot singlehanded around The Solent, but an overnight solo passage was still on my to-do list. I knew what my limitations were and I knew it would be foolhardy to set off out of the familiar sailing grounds of The Solent alone, even though I desperately felt I had something to prove. I went for a long walk to try and figure out how I was going to mainland Europe on my own, feeling disappointed and lost - disappointed because I was supposed to be feeling free, yet in all honesty everywhere I looked was a roadblock or a restraint. My feelings of being lost stemmed from my sacrificing everything for this voyage, and yet here we were and I couldn't even sail across the English Channel - heck - *people could swim across the Channel.*

After a long walk, I sent an email to Johannes, who had always been encouraging and helpful from the beginning. Explaining my predicament, I pitched the idea of him sailing across the Channel with me as a kind of huge favour. Pressing *Send* without great hope (it seemed all my friends were always busy with work, relationships or excuses), I waited. Surprisingly, Johannes soon replied positively and we discussed the details and my new plan to extend the trip by an additional year in Europe, gain more experience and put more money into the sailing kitty. He thought it was a sensible idea and just two weeks later I was in London picking him up at the train station as he wheeled a life raft down the train platform at rush hour. Via email he'd asked if I had a life raft for the boat, which I did, but it was made in the 1980's and I was skeptical, in a jovial *'no worries mate'* kind of way, as to whether it would actually work if required. Johannes insisted on bringing his own life raft for the journey, and in a very German manner, didn't seem too amused by my laissez-faire attitude to our safety.

We eventually arrived at the boatyard, and Johannes looked disappointingly at *Constellation*. After all the work I'd done, *Constellation* still wasn't really up to the kind of standard one might consider adequate for safe ocean voyaging - in fact, to be entirely fair, *Constellation* didn't really look like she was up for sailing from one side of a Swiss lake to another. My work on her had always been rather utilitarian, and nothing was ever done for looks or polish. The decks looked battered and faded, the cockpit was still full of tools and bits of wood, the interior unkempt and chaotic. I'd spent so much time inside my own head, single-mindedly working and focused, it was hard for me to see what everything might look like from the outside. The look on Johannes' face told me it didn't look good. In my meagre defence, it was hard living inside the tiny space you were so avidly working on, primarily focused on making things robust rather than nice looking. At the end of the day, I was also a complete novice, doing everything I could do with a minuscule pub-wage, using borrowed tools and borrowed knowledge from anyone who walked past and would talk to me. In a way, I was disappointed Johannes wasn't happy. I wasn't the kind of person to have heroes, per se, but I did have people I admired for doing what they said they were going to do and Johannes was one of them.

Jack was still committed to working on the documentary of the voyage, tentatively calling and emailing to see how I was doing, probably wondering whether I was really going to do this thing or whether I was just wasting his time. Jack was keen to document this first real voyage aboard *Constellation* and the addition of Johannes, someone who could actually sail, was good for the story arc. A day after Johannes' arrival, Jack turned up from Berlin with a bag full of camera gear. Jack was always in good spirits and I was glad to have familiar friends around me again. His upbeat attitude was a nice antidote to the sometimes stern looks Johannes was giving me. Jack was always fun and always curious and seeing him in person for the first time in months, I began to understand the documentary had become a kind of obsession for him, much like the voyage was for me. I never knew the full details, but from what I understood, Jack had to hustle in his own way to keep making the film: borrowing money off of family to purchase a camera, maxing out credit cards and working sporadically as an editor for German television. Jack had his own adventure in this too.

All three of us were crammed into the boat, eventually departing under the cover of sunrise two days later. The boatyard I'd been tied up had been great, but I also owed them more money than I actually had in my pocket. I'd always paid my bill on time, but in this case, my bill was unfortunately going to have to wait. I kept tight lipped on this indiscretion, being particularly sure not to allow Johannes to get wind of it. He had a very straight down the line personality and wouldn't see this act as a particularly reasonable one... which I totally understood and felt very guilty about. But, at the same time, I also knew I was going to a major city to get a real job and it wouldn't be too long before I was flush enough to pay my debts. So we left at daybreak.

The weather was idyllic as we motored down the river Hamble, our wake perfectly curling away behind us, causing swathes of boats to rock gently, as if they were bidding us goodbye. Perfectly still, with a bright morning sun, we couldn't have left in more beautiful conditions, feeling the happiest I'd felt in months. Everything had been so difficult up to this point. It felt freeing to think that perhaps I was about to actually have some enjoyable sailing with a couple of friends in new and foreign waters. Besides, we were sailing across the English Channel for real this time! Johannes' presence lifted a huge weight off my mind, because sailing for me was still a very anxious activity - I had so much to learn and so much confidence still to build. To have someone else onboard who knew what they were doing and who I could learn from was invaluable.

Constellation may have looked rough, but she was stout and strong, as we sheeted the sails off and headed out towards Brighton without a hitch. I could begin to see Johannes warming to *Constellation*, sensing he was beginning to have more faith in both myself and the boat, as we traded turns at the helm. Our first stop before crossing the English Channel was Brighton, after which we would head to Dover and then across to Ostend in Belgium. While Johannes helmed, I took a mooring line, tied it to the stern and jumped off the boat, letting *Constellation* tow me along in the cold English sea, steaming along under full sail. These were the kinds of moments I'd been waiting for. Up until this point, the sense of freedom I was searching for was nowhere to be seen, everything having felt more like a series of struggles, a whole lot of work and sacrifice, and to be honest, a lot of loneliness. I felt such happiness with *Constellation* sailing slowly but confidently in light winds, her foresail in a goose-wing configuration, dead downwind along the English coast. Johannes said this was the kind of sailing I would eventually be doing within the trade-wind belt en route to the Caribbean, as I imagined azure waters and warm winds.

I used the VHF radio in earnest for the first time, shyly announcing our arrival into the Brighton marina, seeking directions to the visitor berth. We stayed overnight, with Jack leaving the following morning to head back to Berlin for work. The winds weren't favourable for our departure on to Dover, though we worked with what nature provided, in both wind and tide, steadily progressing east past the Greenwich meridian. The meridian was perhaps the most important imaginary navigational aid on earth - we amused ourselves by looking for a red line which might somehow surround the planet as a gift to all sailors. While the prime meridian is a line which exists only in our minds and upon navigational charts, its symbolism struck a deep chord with me as we drifted past the *zero degree* point, marvelling at the GPS as it ticked over.

Passing around Eastbourne, the swell began to increase, as *Constellation* began to surf down the faces under considerable speed. Thankfully the elements were all aligned in the correct direction, but it was easy to see how miserable the voyage could turn if either the wind or the waves were to switch against us. We approached Dover at the 2 mile mark, radioing for permission to enter the Easterly entrance. Port control let us through and we stayed the night at Tidal harbour, the cheapest place we could find without going through closing bridges. Curiously, as we came into port we noticed a set of flagpoles at the entrance, showing the German and Australian flag side-by-side, as I nudged Johannes. Restocking with fuel and food for the voyage across the Channel the next day, we ambitiously planned to sail through the night all the way to Ijmuiden, Holland in a single hop. We sailed out of Dover the next day at 2pm to catch the tide, finally leaving England behind.

As we crossed the traffic separation schemes (imaginary lanes in the water which were designed to manage the sheer volume of traffic transiting the channel), night began to fall, the fear beginning to creep up inside me. I would learn to relish night sailing, rejoicing in the ever changing environment, but for new sailors, darkness seems to bring a sense of dread. Our route was still for Ijmuiden, the horizon lighting up with ship lights as vessels and platforms we couldn't necessarily see in the day became visible by night. Our GPS read over 100miles to go, with an ETA of 30hours. Sitting down below, I attempted to cook pasta, precariously holding the pot of hot water as the boat heeled, becoming a kind of human gimbal. Johannes said everything tasted better at sea, and I must admit, that evening's dinner tasted better than anything I'd eaten in months.

An hour after the sun had completely vanished below the horizon, we began our 2 hour watch system - one slept while one steered and kept an eye on things. It was a strange feeling once Johannes was asleep, I sat huddled in the cockpit as the cold northerlies blew and the plankton began to glow like stars in our wake. The feeling was one of responsibility, for myself, the boat and for Johannes. This sense of self-responsibility was what would become a hallmark of my voyage. At 12am it was Johannes' shift, and I defiantly attempted to sleep in the forecabin where I'd been sleeping in the marina, yet there was simply too much movement in the bow. Moving back into the lee quarter berth, we ended up 'hotbunking' for the rest of the night. Everything was wet, the bunk was soaked along with our clothes. Sleeping essentially consisted of curling up in a blanket of salt water with one's eyes closed and imagining somewhere warm and dry until you nodded off. By 4am the wind had kicked up and *George* the electronic tiller pilot (a small autopilot suitable for short legs, but not a sustainable self-steering solution) Johannes had brought along was having trouble keeping course. Pounding into steep waves, we reefed down the mainsail so *George* was able to maintain course again, yet in doing so our speed had decreased dramatically with the tide. Johannes eventually made the executive decision to redirect into Zeebrugge which wasn't too far away, laying south of Ijmuiden. Back on watch, I was secretly a little pleased we were shaving 10-15hours off of our estimated ETA, as to be honest I wasn't having the most amount of fun. The idea of visiting Belgium was an added benefit - I'd never visited!

Water by this stage was literally pouring through the cabin roof from a broken seal around the solar vent, which had been overlooked because I'd never sailed in conditions where *Constellation* sailed more in the fashion of a submarine than a yacht. There was little to be done while on the move, so I sat my watch out, strapped into my harness, getting dumped on by wave after wave, watching trawlers and the occasional tanker motor past. I was fairly exhausted by the time Zeebrugge was in sight, and Johannes showed his sailing experience by sleeping less than I, maintaining an hourly plot and automatically waking up whenever there was the slightest change in the boat's movement. I was impressed by his tenacity and kept mental notes on everything he did; every tweak of the sail, every tiller pilot adjustment, as well as his strict regimen of keeping tabs on it all. Eventually, we made it into the Royal

Belgian Yacht Club at dawn, Johannes spending the day exploring while I slept like the dead.

While I'd been sleeping, Johannes had decided he needed to go back to Hamburg rather than continue with me to Amsterdam. I was disappointed and immediately worried about how I was going to progress on into Amsterdam alone. I was annoyed and felt stuck, but I also understood. He suggested I sail along the internal canals of Holland rather than venture back into the North Sea, an idea I didn't argue with, my fingers still wet and wrinkled from the night before. Never having looked closely at a chart, I was unaware of how extensive the canal network was inside Europe, particularly Holland. In addition, while the voyage across the channel had been an eye opener, it still didn't feel right to be out there on my own.

The next day Johannes left, and I was back onboard, entirely alone.

AN IMPOSSIBLE START

The route from Vlissingen at the bottom of Holland into Amsterdam was quite practically called *The Standing Mast Route*. The route got its name because a small sailboat could navigate the canals without having to remove or fold the mast to transit under bridges. This entire idea was quite a novelty and completely unplanned, as *Constellation* and I navigated locks and bridges, sailing and motoring through fields and cities. Less than a week before we were pounding away in the North Sea, now here we were pleasantly meandering along. Each night I would sail into a small town, tying up on the town dock or alongside other friendly boats. I was having so much fun that I completely forgot about the harsh realities of sailing out at sea.

With friends visiting for short legs along the way, I eventually made it to Amsterdam in the middle of the night. Holland had displayed an unusual transportation priority, which put people on foot first, then cyclists, then ships, and lastly, cars. This meant, throughout the trip, priority was almost always given to *Constellation* as we needed to transit a lock or have a bridge raised for us to continue. We literally stopped traffic at a moment's notice, as lock and bridge keepers kept us moving along until we reached the outer limits of Amsterdam, where trains appeared to finally take transportation priority. Once per day at midnight, a large bridge which supported both cars and trains had to be lifted for vessels to enter the inner-city. Each night at 11pm, a queue of small boats would circle in anticipation of this major lock & bridge combination to let us pass. After eventually making it through, a series of bridges seemingly opened in front of us, as if by magic, and our group of small boats motored through a midnight chill towards the city centre. It was the most beautiful sight, *Constellation* amongst all these vessels in darkness, pushing along the quiet canals of Amsterdam in unison, the city lights providing enough visibility to see without worry. Eventually we made it to a small marina opposite the central train station of Amsterdam at 2am, where we stayed for the next month trying to figure out what to do next.

The days in Amsterdam flew by as I searched for work half-heartedly and disappointingly looked at the calendar, as winter approached without empathy for my plight. I ended up moored next to a young couple on a boat who were of a similar age to me, who were also stranded and working to save after destroying their engine when a fishing net got caught in their prop late at night. Even though it was August pushing into

September, I still had some tiny hope deep inside my heart, that I could somehow get to the Canary Islands and do my Atlantic crossing that year. It was a ridiculous notion, meaning my Biscay crossing would have to take place in October, or even November - the optimum month being June. I was so obsessed with crossing the Atlantic that season, I simply couldn't let it go, even though I knew it was an insane proposition, and one which many people around me warned against. I'd emailed Johannes with the idea that I still wanted to leave and turn around for more southern latitudes. He warned against it and wasn't happy with the idea. As it would later turn out, people had suggested for Johannes to distance himself from me, thinking I was perhaps pushing the limits of adventure into the outer realm of foolhardiness. They weren't wrong, in hindsight it was madness.

I spent weeks scheming, emailing and talking to people, trying to push anyone who would listen to my dream. My good friend and business partner Marty insisted I have an EPIRB (emergency beacon) onboard if I really was going to leave, and promptly shipped me one out of his own pocket - just one of the many acts of kindness he displayed throughout the voyage. With the help of good friends both old and new, along with the support of windvane manufacturer Windpilot, I managed to purchase the major piece of the puzzle for *Constellation*: the self-steering. As with many critical parts on a boat a sailor affectionately names, I uncreatively named this new piece of gear '*Windy the Windpilot*'. I was now, at least from a technical perspective, fully equipped to sail south. I moved *Constellation* slightly further north to Monnickendam, where I had better access to some metal fabrication facilities I required for mounting the new windvane and promptly installed the gear as fast as I possibly could. The marina had recently been upgrading the docks with newer materials, however the finger I was moored to was still made out of wood. Stuck for some marine-treated mounting plates, I quietly sawed the ends off the end of a dock section as neatly as possible, and carefully worked from the dinghy to mount the gear. Within a matter of days, I turned around and headed back to Belgium, en route to the Bay of Biscay. I left without ceremony in late September, on what I considered to be the official start of the voyage. Paying my bill in Monnickendam, the man behind the desk asked where I was going as a huge squall rattled overhead. I said I was going to Australia. I took a marina brochure as a souvenir and headed off into a mighty rainstorm.

The heavens opened up above us as we motored out into the IJmeer, en route back to Amsterdam. I held a cheap camera out and pointed it back at myself, exclaiming *'here we go'*, the whole spectacle being as unceremonious as heading into the supermarket for bread. It was here that I began to realise that while I had spent a lot of the journey worrying about externalities, such as money, routes, or the people I'd met or the people I might have let down, in reality this trip was really all just in my head. It was all mental. I had set a goal for myself and the reality of it was that it wasn't glamorous or earth shattering or perhaps even entirely unique. It was simply me enacting this big idea I'd had and right at this moment it was actually beginning. In many ways, the lead-up was a lot more exciting than the kind of inane reality of actually doing it. Everything up to that point had been such a distraction, such a thrill, and yet here we were, heading off across a Dutch lake in a squall, to boldly cross oceans in winter, and no one really cared but myself. I often questioned why I was going to so much effort. I thought back to all the old men I'd met along the way who were still preparing for their long voyages. I began to realise that perhaps they had gotten to a point of actually being ready, or, at least ready enough to leave and do the rest on the way, only to have this kind of vertigo I was starting to feel which made them turn around. The invention of more endless jobs, holding onto tenuous commitments, a dozen new reasons not to leave. There is a comfort in preparation - a comfort in mindless work, a comfort in retiring endless ambition for a while just to tinker. The moment I left, I was suddenly faced with myself - the distraction of jobs and the hustle for cash was over - and it was terrifying. Now what? I had to actually go off and risk my life to prove to myself... perhaps also to prove to others that I had the gumption to do what I said I was going to do? Yes, that is exactly what I had to do. And so off we went into the North Sea, battling self-doubt and hoping it would all settle and I'd allow myself to really enjoy the adventure I'd committed to.

The North Sea canal towered above us, this mighty feat of engineering protecting inner-Holland from becoming part of the North Sea itself. The protection of the locks, lakes and canals inside Holland had been calming, however the ocean lay just ahead of this concrete mass in front of us. I was nervous about going back out, thinking back to the night at sea with Johannes. It was colder now, there was a bite in the air which was a constant reminder that winter was just a moment's notice away. The weather was already more unpredictable, I kept a close eye on various forecasts, wondering how quickly I could progress down the western coasts of Europe between bouts of questionable weather windows.

The final lock released us into the sea, and we were off. Before long the shores of Belgium were back, where I made my first stop. I had decided to day-sail for a while, coastal hopping as much as I could while avoiding night passages, until there was no other option. I laid in wait for two days in Ostend, walking along the rather plain beach, realising how lucky I was to come from a country with such a beautiful coastline. The Europeans certainly had their nice buildings and an air of culture on every corner, but I pined for the ruggedness and sense of remoteness I loved in Australia. In a way I was looking for this at sea - there was an inner-obsession with wildness I didn't realise I possessed until now. As I spent my days coastal sailing and thinking, my eyes focused on infinity, interrupted by ships or small glimpses of wildlife and coastline to port.

From Calais, France, I made the pointless decision to hop across to England again, a short sail of only 20 miles to Dover. There was no particular reason for this, I think I just loved the idea of sailing to another country where I could speak the language for a brief moment. Filling up every tank I had onboard with the lower cost marine red diesel in England, my confidence was building with every mile under the keel, as I departed at sunrise the next morning, bound for Fécamp, France. The weather was unexpectedly stable and idyllic. My criss-crossing the Channel being the most enjoyable sailing to date, with *Constellation* sailing confidently under windvane.

While the sailing was going well, my loneliness seemed unending. *Constellation* sailed defiantly under her self-steering, requiring little intervention from me, providing quiet moments to sit on deck and simply watch the water pass under us. This gave way to my maintaining a keen lookout for other sailing boats, signs of life, or just anything to break this impending sense of isolation. No other boats sailed by because the season for it was long gone, and the Channel seemed curiously devoid of life. In a sense, this broad sea presented a mirror into myself, albeit a mirror reflecting back more questions than answers. Truly, this is what I was here for, for these introspective moments to bubble to the surface, no matter how hard they were. I wasn't here to find myself or even become a great sailor (good enough not to die was my ambition). I was here to create myself anew, and at that moment, the sea reflected a lonely ego in constant need of love. This was to be my first glimpse at what was really coming - these critical hours on deck in the Channel laid out the mental and emotional future of the voyage: a very private battle with the self, the ocean and the elements.

The entrance into Fécamp approached, framed by shingle beaches and impressive white cliffs. A town built on Cod fishing, Fécamp was once supported by salting, curing, rope making, fish sales, netting and boat construction. The prosperity of the region rapidly dwindled after the implementation of Newfoundland's cod fishing quotas, drying up the bountiful Canadian fisheries which supported this small village on the other side of the Atlantic (along with many others). Virtually being winter, I tied up alone along the fishing docks, sitting in the cockpit after my Channel crossing, pondering the global effects of the Cod economy, my loneliness and wistfully looking at a chart for my next hop.

Looking closely at the chart, it was clear the next leg was an unavoidable night passage. This was to be my first solo night passage at sea, something I'd been thinking about for a long time. My coastal sailing thus far was making me feel both confident and humble at the same time - perhaps the ideal state of mind for any risky endeavour. The forecast looked good and we set off, passing the striking rock formations of Étretat to our port side. The port city of Le Havre teased me as we passed: I could have stopped and kept my routine of day sailing intact, but we pushed on into the setting sun.

In the cockpit, I nervously watched the sun slowly dip on the horizon. There was a pending sense of doom as the light dwindled uncontrollably, shrinking my tiny floating world even further. *Constellation* moved gracefully along under her own steerage and power, as I hopped below to make food, constantly popping my head up to keep an eye on things. With a tin pot of pasta on my lap, with a jar of pasta sauce stirred in, I rugged up to watch the coastline gradually pass me by, clipping along nicely at 5kts. Once I'd accepted I couldn't stop the sun setting, the night passage started to become enjoyable: I recalled Johannes' joy of night sailing and started to get onboard with the idea.

By midnight I was dozing in the cockpit, *Constellation* still maintaining a good course for Cherbourg. It was now time to try and sleep in earnest while underway. It's difficult to describe the act of sleeping while a boat is sailing itself - the closest way to describe it would be to liken it to driving along the highway in your car, letting the wheel go and climbing into the backseat with a blanket and a pillow - waking up every 20 minutes to make sure you weren't going to veer into a truck.

Laying in my bunk in the lee side of the boat, I nervously tried to sleep. It was impossible. With an egg timer, I would set it to 20 minutes and try my hardest to keep my eyes shut, but I simply couldn't do it. Every 5 minutes I'd be up poking my head into the cockpit just to make sure everything was ok. Because of our proximity to land, solo coastal sailing under windvane is often more dangerous than making open-ocean passages. Land is the arch-enemy of any boat, and the slightest navigational error, sleep-scheduling mistake or change in wind direction (conversely modifying the boats course) could quickly turn disastrous. In the open-ocean, there is usually enough space and leeway to handle small mistakes.

Cherbourg was an uneventful stopover, as I arrived at dawn, tired but very pleased to have successfully achieved my first overnight solo passage. The port was busy with marine traffic, with ferry's headed to England loading cars and passengers as I lay awake in my bunk trying to sleep, still buzzing from being up most of the night sailing. My stops along the coast of Europe were all short and to the point, my mission was to cross the Bay of Biscay as soon as possible. After an altercation in the marina with a creepy middle aged man who was watching me strangely and following my every move, I departed the following day with another several days of fine sailing weather ahead.

I tackled the infamous Race of Alderney, a strait which produces fast and difficult tides, 'racing' at up to 12kts. *Constellation* zoomed along at 7kts and I patted myself on the back for getting my tide calculations correct. Mistakes in these treacherous waters can easily lay a boat up on the rocks, a small vessel such as *Constellation* being no match for racing bodies of water this size. Under full sail, we headed off into the Channel Islands, eventually motoring into Guernsey off the coast of Normandy as the sun set and the winds abated, slipping into St Peter Port without trouble. The whimsical harbour, dotted with small fishing boats is overlooked by a cluster of beautiful white buildings of an almost Parisian nature. From here, one could sail off to the west and not reach land until the shores of Musgrave Harbour, Newfoundland.

I'd sailed to the Channel Islands as a person obsessed with freedom and autonomy, curious to visit a modern day tax haven and former nexus of government-sanctioned piracy. With the islands' close proximity to Europe, the region had developed an autonomous outlook, a culture born from the days of privateering during the 17th and 18th centuries. If only I could apply for a *letter of marque* and run *Constellation* as a privateer vessel! For now I'd have to make do with long walks across cobblestones, counting bank signs and climbing tiny winding staircases as I kept an eye on the enormous tide, the beach drying for hundreds of yards as one of the world's largest tidal ranges worked in silence.

The engine sounded curious as we motored back out of the breakwater the next morning. My stay was brief, the goal of Biscay unending. The sounds a boat makes are akin to practicing an instrument, one's ear develops an expected note for everything: the sound of a flapping sail, water across the hull at differing angles, the thump and particular note of the single-cylinder Diesel engine. Sailing solo is being in a state of constant awareness and connectedness with your boat and your natural surrounds. On our way out, something just didn't sound quite right. As I motored back into the harbour, picked up a mooring and dove over the side in the chilling but clear water, only to discover the propeller wound up with fishing line. A misfortune such as this can easily destroy a marine engine, much like my friends in Amsterdam who were forced to delay their trip by a year after losing their engine to fishing net entanglement.

The sail back to Brittany, France was slower than anticipated, my ill-timing resulting in a night sail up unfamiliar river waters and into Lézardrieux. As if timed for maximum disruption, my only GPS failed without reason. The river sank below impenetrable clouds of fog as we motored past various hazard markers, lights and outgoing traffic. I was furious at myself for navigating with only a single GPS unit onboard, something I kept meaning to resolve but hadn't. I resorted to paper charts, however under the fog it was virtually impossible to make any hard references for which to navigate by. In pure fury I threw the handheld GPS overboard, knowing full well that I should not have been navigating blind up this river while relying only on a single navigational aid. I slowed down to a walking pace, scrambling to the bow and back, trying to see through the fog and make sense of my whereabouts. If I was unable to tie up to something, it was going to be impossible for me to simply stay up all night in a running river - I would have to head back out to sea and put myself on a tack towards Canada and try to get some sleep, then return in the morning when the fog had burned off.

By sheer luck, Neptune granted me both a lesson and a saviour: a small fishing boat was moored just in front of me. Motoring around in circles, I eventually located another mooring which looked safe enough to tie up on. With relief I was secured to the mooring ball and fell asleep in an instant.

The Bretons were known as a fiery and independent bunch who loved the sea, sailing and hearty food. Well, that's what I liked to imagine from reading and talking to people. I awoke to an eeriness as we remained surrounded by a dense fog. Even in broad morning daylight, all I could see was the bow of the Breton fishing boat from the previous night's adventure. Without a GPS and quite literally about 10 metres of visibility, I was at a loss of where exactly I was. There wasn't much I could do but wait for the fog to burn off, so I went down below and read whilst drinking coffee for a few hours until visibility increased. By the early afternoon I could see a small jetty with other sailing boats and decided to sail over and tie up to work out my next maneuver and check on the weather.

I threw my line to some sailors sitting cross-legged on the pier who tied me up, asking in broken English where I was from and where I was going. I sheepishly told them I was sailing to Australia, attempting to explain that the boat was from England and I was now on my way to Melbourne. I always held my cards close to my chest, careful not to appear brazen or boastful, however these joyful sailing Bretons just shook my hand heartily and invited me to join their dockside afternoon lunch.

I was later sent back to *Constellation* after an amazing day of eating and drinking, my arms full with food supplies, apple liqueur and wine. We could barely communicate in a common language, but it didn't matter, we connected over boats, dreams, freedom, the sea and hearty food. The Bretons were just like I imagined. I slept with a smile on my face and woke up to blue skies.

The next day was spent exploring the river at low tide, taking time out to claw oysters off the rocks with a screwdriver. Life was simple and beautiful in Lézardrieux. The following day I left early on a good outgoing tide, navigating by sight, compass and chart into the town of Trebeurden, where I bought a new GPS and fixed a failing alternator.

I looked at my chart nervously, as the wide-open expanse of the Bay of Biscay neared closer and closer to my marked position. It was now mid to late October, with winter approaching like a freight train from the north. Yet, rather curiously, the weather up until this point had continued to be rather spectacular. While most people had put their boats away for winter, I was still out there taking advantage of an unseasonal patch of stable weather, sailing completely alone, not bumping into another sailing boat the entire way from Zeebrugge to Camaret. What did everybody else know that I didn't? Probably a lot, but I wasn't about to start questioning my good fortune as I started to make serious plans about my Biscay crossing.

BISCAY & BEYOND

In Brest, I emailed a good friend and asked if I could borrow $150. I desperately needed to borrow some money to pay a professional weather routing service, in order to route my safe passage across the Bay of Biscay. My friend was obliging and I added his name to the growing list of people I'd borrowed or been given money from. I was internalising a lot of fear for this passage, as it was my first real sailing test and multi-night passage. I'd managed to pass a bunch of other tests along the way, for example, actually getting a boat and making it all the way here without major mishap, but this was different. Hustling on land to make things happen, or coastal sailing had an 'out' if the going got tough - days into a difficult 3-4 day crossing, there is no such option. This was the beginning of my true phase of maximum self-responsibility.

The weather routing service saw no possible windows for a safe crossing within the next 7 day forecast period.

I lay low, burning nervous energy on procrastination in port. For two days I walked. Re-packed the boat. Walked. Made minor repairs. And walked mindlessly along the coast wondering what on earth I was doing. The weather changed everyday, from cold to practically warm, to stormy and back again. I was carrying a lot of self-doubt again, even though I'd been slowly building a confident resolve in myself and *Constellation* over the previous weeks. My incessant nervous walking wasn't helping, it was only making things worse as I piled doubt upon doubt upon myself, questioning what I was doing, where I was going, and most importantly, *why* I was doing any of this at all.

The *why* of this voyage only ever reared its ugly head when I was full of doubt. On the one hand, doubt is a really important trait, and it was one which I believe kept me safe because it kept me questioning. I always felt on edge, never totally confident, yet never completely paralysed by fear either. I had such a huge respect for the ocean, a respect which was rooted in feeling its power and its changeability, but also it was rooted in my own near-drowning as a child, a vivid memory of being pulled into shore by a stranger on a remote Australian beach. Exhausted, I had nothing left as I surrendered to tiredness, letting my body sink to the bottom. My feet eventually touched the sand, and like lightning, an energy deep inside me returned. There lay a dormant fire in my stomach which told me that day was not the day I was going to drown. I pushed off the sandy bottom with a new strength to live, signs of my rescuer paddling towards me.

On the third day, the weather routing service emailed me and said there was a possible window coming up in 3 days. My haze of fear, irrationality and doubt changed gears and I suddenly knew what I had to do: I had to cross the Bay of Biscay, and I suddenly began to know that I could. *Constellation* was a sturdy and proven boat. I was young, I had a ton of energy, and I could turn stress and fear into rational action when required. The *why* became the *how*, as I tore everything out of *Constellation* on the dock to make all those final little repairs, and to finish off all those small jobs I'd been avoiding. There was a goal set in place and I had three days to make sure I was as prepared as I could be.

I left at 4am in full wet weather gear. It was cold, dark and black. My hands shivered on the tiller as we motored out into the void, six jerry cans of diesel strapped either side of the narrow deck. With the sails hoisted, we pointed 210 degrees on the compass and headed out past Pointe du Raz, towards Galicia in Spain. By evening the winds had died off and I became caught in a race around the Pointe, moving nowhere fast. I helmed all night under engine, the self-steering unable to function without any wind, as I worked *Constellation* in breaking away from the tide. For the first time we were completely out of sight of land, the luminous sun rising to an endless view of the ocean all around us. I was delirious from a lack of sleep, becoming frustrated by midday at the lack of wind to properly sail and steer the boat. The weather window I had to make this crossing successfully had one caveat: it *had* to be done within three and a half days. This meant I had to maintain a minimum speed the entire way, with a large low pressure system barreling down from the icy northern latitudes, heading towards me without compassion.

On my second night having gone virtually 24 hours without sleep, ship lights began appearing on the horizon. Or were they? Then more appeared. Dozens of lights, *everywhere.* I was delirious from sleep, taking my jacket off to force the cold into my bones and keep me awake. In my delirium this seemed like a good idea. The shipping lights were confusing and before long I was surrounded by fishing trawlers. They were displaying unusual motoring lights which I didn't immediately recognise (ships display lights as a pattern for other seamen to discern the nature of the ship and its possible movements). Flipping through a small book on shipping lights, I identified them as pair trawlers. These ships work in unison, side by side, separated by a large trawling net. I soon realised I could quite easily sail right into the middle of two ships towing these enormous nets. The fleet became larger and larger, my confusion grew, and eventually I gave up trying to navigate my way around them all. I had never felt so utterly exhausted in my life, and the more tired I got the less I cared about anything: except sleep. I cared more than anything about sleep. I envisioned the storm chasing me, its life beginning somewhere north of Spitsbergen, raging down the North Sea and into the Bay of Biscay, where it would hurl me into the shore, turn me upside down, or torment me to the point of voluntarily throwing myself overboard, just to make it all go away.

The second day provided enough wind for the self-steering to just barely function. I slept in 20 minute blocks in the cockpit, waking up to ensure we were headed in the right direction and the horizon was clear of other ships. I gripped the kitchen timer on my chest with two hands, battling my inner willpower with every alarm, my body telling me to go back to sleep, attempting to trick me into sleeping, my mind insisting the opposite. Every 20 minutes I would wake up disoriented and wondering what on earth I was doing. Every 20 minutes it was the same battle and internal dialogue:

"Don't get up."
"You need to get up."
"It doesn't matter, what is life anyway?"
"Where are you?"
"Who's idea was this?

To win a battle is one thing, but to win a battle with yourself every 20 minutes takes a whole other kind of energy.

Eventually the coast of Galicia was near. As the continental shelf re-appeared undersea, a lone dolphin darted around us, its torpedo-like wake lit up in bio-phosphorescence. I ran up to the bow to watch, laughing with joy at the gift I'd been awarded for overcoming myself, if only for a second. Suddenly I had a brief moment of realisation, that all this inner fear and turmoil was wasteful and immature. My fears were outwardly directed at the ocean, the weather and my progress. But none of those things possessed fear, reacted to fear, or were motivated by fear. Everything I had battled with over the last three days and built up inside my head was a completely one-sided battle made up in my own mind. It was strange to think of the whole ordeal as a battle of sorts - a battle where only one side of the fight is chomping at the bit, while the other side is entirely nonplussed: I had realised a vital lesson - the sea, the air, the sun and the deep-seated stars were not necessarily uncaring of my plight, they just displayed their neutrality of existence. A neutrality I could dare learn from. The winds acted as themselves and the ocean rose as crests and sunk into troughs, ad infinitum, without question, hesitation, or self-doubt. It was me that was acting out of line in this divine order. What was I supposed to do? What was my role in amongst all this nature, all this reality I had set myself into, completely alone?

I navigated into the bright lights of La Coruña in the northwest region of Galicia, Spain, fumbling around the docks and eventually finding a vacant pontoon to tie *Constellation* up against at 3am. A boat at sea is a constant source of inescapable noise, with everything creaking, slapping, whining or something in between. All these noises make up the song of sailing, and I'd learned how important it was to listen to the song, because it told you stories. I recalled a book by Bruce Chatwin called 'The Songlines', which talks about how indigenous Australian people would navigate across otherwise impassable deserts by song, each rhythm and each phrase helping them traverse the landscape, the memory of geography embedded within each musical motif like a migratory bird. The songs sung by *Constellation* gave me little in the way of navigational information, either because they didn't contain such data, or because I wasn't at a point where I could interpret it. What I did understand of her song, though, gave me a constant status on the boat and the conditions we were in. From the sound of the water upon the hull, particular creaks only certain motions generated or the slaps of wind on her sail, provided small but detectable hints about our progress and our safety. By the third night at sea, even the smallest deviations in this song would raise my attention, and later, on longer passages, the smallest differences in its phrasing could wake me from even the deepest slumber. This connectedness with *Constellation* was unlike any other passage so far, and I could see it took a certain amount of non-stop time at sea to get into a certain kind of intuitive state.

I woke up the next morning at 10am sharp, a hard knocking on the hull making me jump. I looked out the companionway to see a stern man talking swiftly at me in Spanish, motioning that I must come to the office with great urgency. I tried to explain I'd just sailed all the way from France in this tiny boat alone and I would come to the office later. He persisted. I wanted to tell him I'd been up all night and had the most extraordinary transcendental experience, watching a dolphin in the phosphorescence like a torpedo lit by a trail of fireworks. I wanted to express my realisation that all my fear didn't really exist anywhere but inside myself and it *wasn't even real!* I wanted to express how the distant and existential stars made me feel infinitesimal yet alive and full of hope. I wanted to desperately share all of these discoveries, but really the dock master was just trying to explain that it was 12 euros a night and I needed to come fill out some paperwork now, not later.

On the walk back to *Constellation*, a 40ft yacht was towed in by the *Civil Guardia*, its rudder broken, sails strewn across the deck, the crew looking weathered and relieved. As predicted, the front from the north had arrived, just 12 hours after my safe arrival into La Coruña. Unbeknownst to me, this yacht was on a similar track to me, only half a day behind. *Constellation* and I had dodged the front, my tireless helming and seemingly endless battle for southerly progress through the Bay had been worth every struggle.

Amongst the pontoons, I befriended a Dutch family with three kids. The father was a tugboat captain, specialising in towing difficult equipment across entire oceans, living aboard their small yacht, the father flying off to remote locations to perform dangerous work, before returning and carrying on with their comparatively leisurely cruise along the coast of Europe. They were kind to me, I played with the kids, we built rafts and threw them into the marina, much to the chagrin of the dock master. They felt pity for my parents for having their son out here alone sailing on a small boat and gifted me an old but fully functional satellite phone for the rest of my voyage.

The further I sailed, the more I had to come to terms with the generosity of others and what it meant. By this point I really had nothing left, financially. I met one young sailor who was quite literally eating mussels off the marina wall in order to eat, and I thought back to my days in Berlin sleeping on a piece of cardboard, collecting plastic bottles to change out into supermarket vouchers. What made people do this? What was making *me* do it? And why were people responding with generosity so I could keep going? It was humbling, perplexing and beautiful. In some ways I was doing what a lot of people perhaps dream of doing, giving it all up for a life-changing adventure. People can recognise adventure and they can recognise gusto and in a way I suppose it's a rare trait. It wasn't something I was aware of then, I was simply pig-headed on doing what I said I was going to do, sometimes feverishly fighting the urge to throw it all in and join the Plum Village monastery in nearby Bordeaux. In fact, I came so close at one point, I emailed the monastery to find out whether I could arrive with nothing, visions of intentionally sinking the boat so as to meditate and find peace in another more knowable way. They said yes to my query, but thankfully their response took a week which was enough for me to re-align my wavering internal compass.

The generosity of others was one of the keys, both practically and emotionally, to my continued southerly efforts towards the Canary Islands, with winter now well into season. At the beginning of the voyage I was battling my own inner dialogue to continue on. Yet, as the generosity piled up, so too did a sense of external obligation. On the one hand I couldn't continue without other people, but on the other hand this was supposed to be about freedom, autonomy, adventure and fortitude. I struggled intellectually in a sense with this idea, yet my heart sung with gratitude at this communal recognition of my boundless desire to keep going against all odds. It would be false to say I was doing this for others, yet the somewhat public nature of the voyage did keep me accountable on those dark days when it all seemed futile.

THE KINDNESS OF STRANGERS

Time ticked by in La Coruña, each day accruing against my marina bill. A month went by, and all of a sudden I didn't have enough money to pay and leave. My days in La Coruña were simple, with coffee in the mornings and an endless search for work by day and night. By the end of the second month, I'd managed to secure enough remote freelance programming work to pay my way out and continue south. The work was tedious and low paying, but work in Spain itself was virtually non-existent so I was happy I could at least do something.

I had many unexpected adventures in La Coruña, from a tour of another Contessa 26 owner's family vinegar factory, lunches in a country club and coffee with a man who used to greet OSTAR racers and invite them to his house for dinners and showers. He said I had 'tiny thin legs, like all small boat sailors' (occurring of course because of a lack of anywhere to use a pair of legs on such a small boat!). The friendly waitress at the nearby German-named 'Guesthof' cafe couldn't speak a word of English, but took a liking to me and waved at the dock before generously handing me 100 euros for my trip. She wrote a letter in Spanish which a friend translated, where she exclaimed that she was glad that I was not a 'Pijo'. My translating friend laughed and said it meant she was glad I wasn't a "conformist middle-class snob" like many others who sail into town, wearing "tweed, Burberry, Barbour and such, looking like they have just come off a stag hunt in Scotland."

As a storm barrelled towards me, I sought refuge in the fishing village of Laxe, a short sail out of La Coruña en route to Portugal. I had a photocopied cruising guide for the area, clearly marked with a jetty I could tie up on. Searching everywhere to make sense of the area, I nearly crashed into a well marked outcrop of rocks as I navigated via GPS, the jetty apparently now non-existent. Pulling in behind the breakwater wall, I motored around in circles, wondering what to do, there being no obvious place to anchor or tie up, except on the wall itself. Some fishermen whistled me over to a ladder, telling me to come up, pointing at the dark lines across the northern horizon. Putting all the fenders out, I climbed the ladder, with half a dozen men trying to talk to me in Spanish. Understanding virtually nothing, one of them went into town and came back with an Englishman who translated what I was doing out here: *I'm sailing this small boat I bought in England to Australia.* Before long, the Englishman brought over another fisherman, who insisted I tie *Constellation* up to a mooring ball for the next three days, as a large weather system was arriving. Confused, I got back onto *Constellation* with the fisherman and he tied me up alongside an old fishing boat inside the protected harbour. Another fisherman came out on a small tender, and took us both to shore, as I tried to explain that if I left *Constellation* how would I get back? From what I could understand he said I couldn't stay on the boat, as it was too dangerous. I soon gave up trying to understand and took a few essentials in a backpack.

The Englishman introduced me to his cousin who only spoke Spanish. Translating backwards and forwards, I understood they were a fishing family who wouldn't let me sleep on my boat through the storm, explaining that I would stay with them. I couldn't protest as I was led down some laneways and up two flights of stairs to an apartment overlooking the harbour, where I could see *Constellation* bobbing away in the calm before the storm. It turned out I wasn't to stay with anyone at all, I was actually given an unoccupied apartment all to myself to stay in for the next three days! Sitting on the kitchen bench watching the storm roll in, I heard a knock on the door. Someone's grandma stood on the stairs holding a large pot of something, motioning I take it. I took the pot off her, after which she reached into her apron pockets and pulled out two cans of beer, placing them on top of the pot, before turning around and walking back down the stairs. Dumbfounded by such generosity, I sat at the table watching *Constellation* as the sun set over a delicious Spanish stew and beer.

The next morning, the old grandma of Laxe appeared with a huge potato frittata, bread and milk. I was floored by the town's generosity, as I spent my day meandering up amongst the enormous hills, peering southwest in the direction I would soon be sailing again. At night I would try watching Spanish television which seemed loud and obnoxious. I'd managed to get back onto *Constellation* briefly, so I picked up some books and charts to study while the weather improved. Reading a Webb Chiles book, I felt a strong connection in his words:

"To me a voyage is essentially an act of will and a testing of the human spirit. If a sailor doesn't learn anything more important from the sea than how to reef a sail, the voyage wasn't worth making. One of the pleasures in setting out on a voyage is not knowing where the sea will lead. On a voyage a sailor is at risk. On a voyage a sailor knows he is truly alive. A voyage is not an escape from life; it is a reach for life."

In essence Chiles was touching on the words of Shaw: *"Life isn't about finding yourself. Life is about creating yourself."* For me, this voyage was not an escape - a simple assumption I'd heard on more than one occasion - it was the simple act of working to create and better oneself. Perhaps in hindsight, it was even a latent and self-imposed initiation ceremony - to shift from boy to man. Unexpectedly along this path of self-creation was the recurring discovery of kindness and generosity - for what better lesson to learn on an initiation than the profound beauty in strangers helping you succeed for completely selfless reasons.

The three days of comfort were soon gone, my stay in Laxe had been tremendously rejuvenating both physically and mentally, being able to sleep on a comfortable bed which wasn't moving about, being fed good food, and feeling a sense of being cared for after such a long time eating cheaply and spending so much time alone. I felt a pang of sadness because I couldn't express myself fully because of the language barrier, saying 'gracias' over and over, using my hands any which way I could to indicate just how grateful I was.

Around the corner from Laxe lay the Spanish Rías, a beautiful granite coastline etched into the Spanish cliffs by millenia of Atlantic waters shifting and moving without a pause. Each Rías, while individual, shares the common characteristic of jutting inland to meet a river, making a glorious ground for sailing and exploring. While picturesque on the chart, I sailed with caution, bold italics naming this region *Costa da Morte* (Death Coast), its waters full of wrecks and the spirits of sailors. Thought of as the 'end of the earth' in Roman times, Cape Finisterre was passed by the Phoenicians on their trade route with Bronze Age Britain, which I marvelled at as little *Constellation* and I lay anchor within the first of the sheltered Rías. While rounding the Cape, I experienced what would be a notable occurrence along the entire voyage, which was entirely unexpected: The smell of each new landfall, should the winds be right. As we slowly motored into port after a pleasant and uneventful rounding of the Cape, I was surrounded by the smell of earth and fried fish. I sat down on the bow of *Constellation*, looking high up onto the mountainous Cape, which was also the end point for a common walking pilgrimage across the north of Spain. While I was too far away to witness it directly, tradition leads pilgrims to burn their clothes and boots at the end of their journey, in celebration and ritual of their achievement. I pondered this over the smell of fish & chips, my head awash with images of great storms, naked pilgrims and great Phoenician ships, undoubtedly anchored at one point in time in the very spot *Constellation* and I rested.

Autumnal Europe served spectacular sunsets and crisp blue-skied mornings, the Rías providing a calm anchorage to wake up to, surrounded by still, glassy waters. For fun, I'd set off the anchor under full sail, each morning, silently exiting anchorages as *Constellation* carved her way further south, dolphins arriving to pilot us into our next port. As we sailed into Sanxenxo by night, the entire town disappeared from sight. Without a moon, the town experienced a short power outage, making the city vanish into darkness. Somewhat perplexed but undeterred, the city re-appeared soon after, which I explored the next morning, buying olives and patatas bravas.

Baiona was the last port of my explorations within the Rías, as well as a major milestone for me on the voyage. It was impossible to always be thinking of my final goal of Australia, the distance and number of challenges to come were too great to manage and consider every single day. In order to manage the length and complexity of the voyage, I slowly learned to mentally break down the voyage into major milestones, Baiona being one of them. I stayed in a marina for the night, the previous day becoming somewhat hectic on the water, with unexpected winds and tides kicking up and forcing me off-anchor to seek more sheltered waters. Grateful to have easy access to the shore, I put my starboard shoe on, only to find it full of coffee from when everything flew across the cabin just hours before. It's hard to express just how quickly life on a small boat can change.

I received a lot of email and comments via my website, one of them being from a Portuguese sailor of a similar age to me, named Pedro. He invited me to Christmas with his family, which I accepted with happiness, swiftly recalling the previous Christmas aboard *Constellation* while still on the hard and under repair in England, burning tea candles to keep warm and shivering the day away, alone. The coast of Portugal was unlike the southern west coast of Spain. This part of the coast had virtually no anchorages, and entrances into marinas or ports were often across dangerous sandbars. As it was now officially winter, I looked nervously at the charts trying to work out how I could get *Constellation* into a port for Christmas. Eventually I chose the small town of Figueira da Foz, motoring slowly and cautiously to the bar edge under a pink sky and an enormous full moon. One in ten waves is statistically twice as high as the other nine, and naturally while I pondered on this thought, wave number ten picked me up and uncontrollably surfed me into the marina. Terrified, I held onto the tiller with both arms, fighting to keep a straight and tight line through the entrance. *Constellation* was a tiny boat, but her long keel and relative weight to size ratio made her pull hard under speed. I tied up in the deserted marina, my hands shaking from the adrenaline and the cold. I'd never met Pedro before, only exchanging emails here and there, yet it didn't deter him from driving the 100km to pick me up and take me to his family home for Christmas.

The Christmas I knew from my childhood was very American, where we all woke up early on Christmas morning, pestering our parents to open presents, followed by a big breakfast of bagels, cream cheese and smoked salmon. The Christmas celebrated in Portugal was much more like a party, with less focus on present giving and more focus on family and celebration. Celebrations began on the 24th of December, with Cod casserole, steamed Cod with potatoes, Turkey, and a range of sweets to rival a bakery. We stayed up virtually the entire night of Christmas Eve into Christmas Day morning, drinking, talking and listening to people play various instruments.

After all this eating and drinking and being part of such an amazing and warm family for several days, I came back to *Constellation* and suffered a full day and night of rather severe 'sailors blues'. On several occasions along the way, my energy and drive would come crashing down, with life taking a temporary but rather serious turn for the worse. I was trapped in Figueira da Foz due to tides and a difficult exit, the small town virtually asleep over the holiday period. This quietness and frustration in my inability to leave lulled me into a deep depression, touching the very core of what it is I'm doing and why. My normally stoic solitude was confused by this outpouring of kindness and family - in the sense that it begged me to ask myself what was really important in life. My family back in Australia was kind and generous, but it was small and didn't have the same kind of warmth I was experiencing in these Southern European countries. For the last couple of months I'd been living so on edge, with such a strong focus on pushing forward, I'd probably really forgotten how miserable my daily life often was. I was extremely lonely, very exposed to the elements and under constant mental pressure and worry from the changing and often harsh weather. Because of the pushing winter, the chance to really sink in and enjoy my surroundings was limited, always having to move on. I was often so in the zone, I didn't really realise how hard things were in reality until I experienced the complete opposite: Whether it be a few nights of warmth and a nice bed in Laxe or the kindness of strangers in Portugal.

Eventually the tides (both figuratively and emotionally) turned and a small weather window pushed me back out into the Atlantic. It was important mentally for me to keep going, that was clear - too long alone without progress led me into dark places. It was becoming apparent how much less alone and more connected with the world I felt when I was in the wild, nature being my antidote to melancholy. A pattern began to emerge with every stop - any more than a day or two of rest and I'd be swept up in a kind of seaport-sadness.

I stopped briefly in Peniche before hopping directly to Cascais, Lisbon. The trip from Peniche was not without its difficulties. For some peculiar reason, I was absolutely beset with boredom. I could not entertain myself in any form, becoming incredibly agitated. No book could hold my attention, no endlessly meditative gazing at the ocean could quell my angst. I saw a bunch of small crabs which seemed to be floating just under the surface, tacking around in circles attempting to catch one with the boat hook just for something to do. This was a fruitless exercise, akin to trying to scoop a single noodle out of a wave pool with a single chopstick. I soon gave up and pushed on into Cascais, docking under sail, my engine refusing to start. The Portuguese authorities weren't convinced with my insurance policy (or lack thereof) and I spent an hour convincing them I was insured but simply didn't have the latest policy in-hand (this was a fib, I couldn't afford the renewal). I eventually tied up and slept peacefully in the protection of the marina.

New Years Eve was soon upon us and I caught up with Pedro in Lisbon, eating prawn curry and taking walks through Lisbon city under fireworks and celebration. It was the eve of the ban on smoking indoors, which of course led everyone who smoked (and those who didn't, including me) to defiantly fill the alleys and corridors of Lisboa with plumes of tobacco smoke. I stumbled across a statue of one of my favourite writers, Fernando Pessoa, and chatted with him for awhile on the topic of banality and the soul, after which I carried on with celebrating another year closer to an all-eventual end.

THE CANARY ISLANDS

Storms railed against the breakwater in Cascais, their collective momentum compounding over hundreds of miles of sea travel before abruptly hitting the wall right near *Constellation*. Occasionally a large set wave would break hard enough to send heavy sea-spray across the decks, making nights in bed sound as if we were actually sailing rather than safely tied up. As the spray hit the decks, my mind recoiled at the prospect of having to leave this place and head back out to sea. It was a ten day sail to the calmer and kinder latitudes of the Canary Islands, but I still had to find a weather window out of Lisbon in between the cold January storms.

I became terribly sick for close to a week, unable to do any jobs on the boat or even contemplate leaving. I lay in bed listening to the weather and feeling sorry for myself. I met another friend also named Pedro, who kindly let me sleep on his couch for a few days to stay out of the cold, which undoubtedly sped up my recovery. Now well into January, the best weather window I'd seen in weeks began to show itself on the forecasts. I began to re-provision in earnest, made repairs to the engine and said my goodbyes. On exiting, I received a stern warning from the Lisbon coast guard that the swell was in excess of 5meters (16ft) and growing steadily. I thanked them for the warning and assured them I knew what was coming. The swell was large, I knew this much, however the wind was consistent for the next three days, giving me enough push to fling me down into more predictable and calmer latitudes off of the African coast. As we chugged out of the protected breakwater, the swell began to lift and heave as *Constellation* hobby-horsed her way out to sea. Having just been sick and on land for several weeks, I braced myself for the coming 24 hours which I knew would surely be hell. Holding onto the mast I raised the mainsail which I'd pre-prepared in port, quickly bringing *Constellation* into a more forgiving motion. A pilot boat cheekily surfed past the entrance at great speed on an incoming wave, leaving a huge wake for me to contend with. I was instantly seasick, vomiting over the rail, with one hand weakly on the tiller. On the upside, the wind was steady both in strength and direction as predicted, allowing me to be sick and not have to contend with the boat as we sailed under windvane. I dozed a little throughout the night, but mostly I lay awake, doing regular checks and trying my best to think of nothing rather than my own self-imposed pity.

My mood seemed directly correlated to the weather,

like a mirror reflected against the sea. As the breeze corrected and the seaway smoothed out, I listened to a lot of Simon & Garfunkel (*'Homeward bound, I wish I was...'*), and the particularly fitting track *'I am a rock'* (*'I am a rock, I am an Island...'*) while enjoying some thoroughly excellent sailing for the first time in a long while. It wasn't to last, but I was far enough offshore not to have to worry about a precise course, enjoying the beauty of the Atlantic Ocean as it glassed over and sparkled in the moonlight. There was no easy way for me to access weather information, so I took what came with close to a thousand miles ahead of me. The fear of becoming becalmed and stuck out here for weeks on end without wind became a more terrifying prospect than heavy weather. I carried only enough diesel to get in and out of port, my progress and the rest of the trip was now entirely up to how the wind blew and the sea swayed.

Radio signals tend to propagate better at night, providing a strong signal from the BBC, where I eagerly listened for the shipping forecast. The famously mesmerising forecast was mostly too general and unhelpful for a small boat such as mine. But I was here, barreling along in this tiny British ship, listening to the BBC under a full moon and feeling absolutely incredible. The wind was variable, staggering our forward progress and forcing me into regular sail changes. Initially a 4am sail change was frustrating, my foresails being hank-on (individual brass clips holding the sail to the stay) and each hank having a tendency to jam. With each change, I'd secure myself to the foredeck, often being dunked on the bow, wrestling the sail down onto the deck. Some of the hank pistons would come off cleanly, while others required a strong pull with rusty pliers. I'd reverse the entire procedure and hoist the sail again to keep us moving along. I began to notice as the days went by, these normally tiresome and frustrating jobs began to lose their annoyance as I hit my rhythm. This was my life. These were my jobs, and I accepted them. I could wake at a moment's notice without feeling groggy or angry, simply shifting from sleep-phase to work-phase, without really even thinking about it, as if the two were connected and harmonious. This lengthier passage was getting me into the mindset I'd been seeking all along - the coastal sailing thus far, kept breaking up my ability to really get into the zone, hindering my ability to reach new mental states. By the fifth day I was living in an almost time-less existence. My work and my time was governed by a higher power - nature. I responded as I was required, my moments no longer regimented by man-made banalities or man-made notions of time.

For the first occasion in my life, I began to feel as though time itself didn't exist. From a young age I have always felt pulled by time, being very aware of how little we have on earth, possessing a strong sense that it could all end at any moment. I remember sitting in the back seat of my parents car, looking out the window at age 14, watching a bird fly parallel to us. For whatever reason, this moment triggered a deep existential sense that life was immensely short, and from that moment on I've had a recurring and deep feeling that I'm not using my time well or the time I have used was not for anything exceptional. Some of this errant fear around time was certainly driving this adventure, and deep in my heart I could feel part of my motivation was a deep sense that I must do something important (to me) with my allotment. My reasons for this voyage were complex and it's part of the reason why I had so much difficulty explaining to people why I was doing it. The whole voyage was attributable to a range of internal impulses - a desire for something wild, raw, and rich with natural beauty. A desire to be immersed and travel wholly and live within new dimensions. To exist in a liminal space which had a higher order, well beyond myself as an individual. The solo aspect was a search to create a self without the cultural baggage of my man-made surrounds - to let the order of nature and her teachings be absorbed untainted. I sought risk as a means to push myself into the moment, for what could be more real than the prospect of death?

Constellation was sailing like a dream. Despite her size, she was sailing along in the middle of the ocean without providing the slightest hint that she wasn't meant to be there. Her long keel gave immense directional stability, her displacement in the water providing a predictable movement, making one feel inherently safe regardless of the apparent insanity of it all upon closer inspection. On more than one occasion, I woke up to find *Constellation* positively flying at over six knots. I'd jump out of my bunk with the full intention of de-powering her, but after getting out of the cabin and sitting on the deck under the mainsail, the sparkling moon and stars would capture my attention. I'd sit down and watch with exhilaration as we cut through the water in the middle of the night, not another soul to be seen, rapt in utter solitude. The moon was large and bright, sometimes making it feel like daylight outside, the water shining a cold silver, *Constellation's* wake a bright white. The stars were bright, beautiful and existential, the moon exuding a somewhat friendly and calming balance to the overhead order of things.

Apart from a small breakage on the main track which led to some amateur fixes with spare bits of halyard, we sailed without problems. My GPS was a small handheld unit, used only for gaining and marking my position on paper charts, which were often hand-me-downs from sailors I met in ports throughout mainland Europe. I had no means to generate power onboard other than with the engine, which I'd run periodically to charge the batteries for our night lights. I pondered a lot on how simple and how enjoyable this passage had become. I'd met so many people who thought I was crazy along the way, laughing on the inside at my boat, at my apparent naiveté and my lack of resources and equipment. This had at times made me second-guess myself - these outside voices often shook my confidence. In one sense, it was good; it ensured that I didn't become arrogant or fool-hardy. But on the other hand, a lot of the skepticism was really other people's stuff, not mine. It was on this passage that I began to truly appreciate the simplicity and low-key nature of my trip and of my choices. Certainly, I had many missing luxuries, but they were exactly that: luxury. What did I really need? I needed a boat that moved forwards, some food, some water, and a way to ensure our forward direction was taking us to the right spot. I had no tangible debt, a little bit of cash, this beautiful little boat and a shelf full of books. For once in my life I felt truly happy, right to my core.

My happiness at sea lasted several days before the anxiety of land made its way across the ocean and into the confines of my little floating universe. The wind swung onto the nose making progress difficult. With Gran Canaria and Tenerife slowly getting larger on the horizon, my anxiety grew with every mile of slow progress. I began to exhaust my very limited diesel reserves so as not to miss the entire island group.

The entry into Gran Canaria is very simple. Yet, when you've been all alone pondering the nature of the cosmos aboard a tiny ship for the last nine days, even the most simple and practical of entries becomes a maze of confusion. Night had fallen and the port was busy with lights and ferry traffic. I contemplated turning around and heading back out to sea for the night, attempting my entry the next morning when I could actually see properly, but I was so wound up with stress I decided to push on and enter. I tied the tiller hard to port so *Constellation* would motor in circles, and went down below to study my charts and make appropriate route markers. How a port looks during the day has virtually no bearing on what it might look like at night. Darkness tends to turn everything two dimensional - it's extremely difficult to judge depth. When sailing into a small city, the lights of the city itself also add to the confusion against the navigational aids. Most small boat sailors would be navigating using a chart plotter, being able to see a clear, top-down version of their progress through the breakwater. I had no such luxury, navigating by eye using old charts which probably only had half the markers I could see. Eventually my location clicked as I lined up a building with the entrance from the main port into the non-commercial marina.

Tying up at the visitor pontoon, it was 2am as I sat in the cockpit after a successful and joyful passage of 10 days. My stress from the night entrance was soon replaced with a deep wave of disappointment. This was not my expected emotion. I expected perhaps elation or a sense of achievement, I suppose. But none of those feelings arose. My beautiful, vast, expansive and self-contained life at sea, where I'd ponder, read, sail and think, seemed to be suddenly and rudely interrupted by landfall.

While passage making was most certainly sublime, there was also an undercurrent of ongoing stress and fear at sea, simply because the environment was also harsh, dangerous and very much predicated on luck. Luck in sailing as well as life is something no one really wants to talk about - this pervasive ideal that everyone is pulling themselves up by their bootstraps. The truth is, solo sailing is a dangerous activity wrought with risk - one missed watch due to sleep, a tiny misstep on deck, or the biggest killer of all: falling overboard while peeing. It can happen, and you sign up for it when you leave the safety of port alone in a boat of any size. Much of life is about how we decide to expose ourselves to risk

- a juggling act, I suppose, of risk versus reward. Whether it's in sailing, love or business, we are constantly analysing our place in it all: What am I risking and what do I stand to gain? Solo sailing has an extremely high exposure to risk, which can increase or decrease dramatically depending on the boat, its size, your equipment and overall experience. However, even amongst all the vectors of vulnerability and risk management, the enormous elephant in the room remains the somewhat difficult acceptance of blind luck.

Because of this, while on passage, even amongst the joyous moments, there is an undercurrent of anxiety in understanding how exposed you are to mishap. The disappointment I was experiencing at 2am on the dock was about living on edge for 9 days and suddenly having all that tension released. If the passage had been done with others, I think elation and excitement would have been the overbearing emotion. Solo, however, the feeling centred on relieving 200+ hours of internalised tension. In addition, this almost transformative experience out in the ocean, amongst all that raw wildness, had come to an abrupt end. In the end, while I was being transformed, the world was still up to its usual tricks: noisy, messy, full of people, polluted and taken for granted. At sea I'd appreciated every nuance for what it was, living in a kind of immediate and beautiful present. Even though it was quiet and most everyone was asleep, the mania of so-called 'reality' hit home. I imagined what it must be like for a baby being born, living in a spectacularly cosy water-world, only to be thrown on to an operating table. I felt a bit like that.

Stepping off *Constellation* onto the dock, I immediately felt land-sick. I swayed around a little as I walked up the pontoon, looking at all the enormous yachts, *Constellation* literally minuscule in comparison, sails strewn across her decks as I hadn't yet tidied up. By now it was around 3am, but I wasn't tired, having lived a weird 24/7 existence for over a week. Stumbling back to *Constellation* there wasn't much else to do other than sleep, with nothing requiring my attention (no sail changes, no course corrections, no watches), so I curled up on an alarmingly still and level bunk. It took another full hour before I could sleep, unable to get used to the calm and quiet.

At 9am sharp the Spanish harbourmaster rudely knocked on my cabin and pointed to the marina office for registration and payment. I sprung up like a cat and bolted out of the companionway as if we'd found ourselves on a lee shore only yards before impact. Alas, it was just another bureaucrat. The Spanish adore their paperwork perhaps even more than the Germans. Again, I had to prove *Constellation* was insured, which she wasn't, but I'd planned for this and forged up to date paperwork in Photoshop a few weeks before. I couldn't afford real insurance, so what was a sailor supposed to do - give up sailing? Endless signatures were required, as I signed each bit of paper with an alternating signature out of boredom. I was in the EU, on an EU boat, with an EU passport, how much of this was *really necessary?* Border control was always so quaint, because it was also so obvious how made-up it all was. If you wanted to do something nefarious it would be so simple, the checks and balances were beyond trivial. The whole process was made even more painful by all its cracks.

Moored amongst brethren, *Constellation* fit into the 'under 35ft and temporary' class of berth, which meant I was suddenly next to people like me: essentially, poor people on yachts with big dreams. *PERFECT.* It was a relief to be amongst my own kind. To my starboard was a young couple awaiting a small child on an old wooden French ship, its interior looking like a tent from the nomadic *Bedouin*. To port was Paul, a hilarious local Canarian about my age, living aboard an old catamaran. Without fail, I could have sworn a different woman climbed out of the centre hatch of his boat every morning. He was hilarious and friendly and I felt like I was at last amongst friends, after a long and lonely battle with the elements along the coast of mainland Europe. The weather had finally warmed up, with sunny days and warm nights, a constant reminder from nature with steady tradewinds, sometimes covering the decks with sands from the sub-Saharan desert. After a solid rest and finding my people, everything was great. The elation and sense of achievement finally arrived, as I watched the sun across the island.

My friend Jack who had started filming the documentary on my voyage managed to perfectly time his arrival into Gran Canaria the next day. It was an absolute joy to see a familiar face after all this time. Jack was in high spirits as always and we spent the following week exploring the island, talking and philosophising.

Jack would film and ask me provocative questions about the trip to try and trigger me into saying something insightful, which sometimes worked and other times led to nonsensical ramblings. Jack soon hugged me and departed after a week of filming in Gran Canaria.

I spent my days planning my Atlantic crossing and mingling with unusual characters I couldn't seem to help myself from bumping into. One morning while at the local cafe borrowing Internet, a German backpacker asked if I had a boat and whether I would sail him to La Palma. I explained that I did have a boat, but it was an extremely small one. Gran Canaria was a hotspot for boat hitch-hikers. In fact there was a beach where they all slept, spending their days plying message boards and the docks looking for crew opportunities to get across the Atlantic. On most days, I'd be asked whether I was crewing for someone and if they could get onboard - I'd respond that I had my own boat, and then spend the next 10 minutes explaining that they couldn't come.

I wasn't interested in sailing to La Palma, although I mentioned I'd consider sailing to La Gomera, where I'd heard stories of hippies living in the sides of caves which lit up at night with candles. The German was uninterested in my counter-offer, but I let him stay in my boat that night as he was tired of sleeping on the beach. The following night we went driving with my marina neighbour Paul, the German requesting to be dropped off at a dense patch of woods. He left me a bag full of mung beans which he asked me to sprout in his absence, rolled a cigarette out of what appeared to be dried flowers, and walked into the forest. We left him and he appeared a few days later at the boat asking about how his beans had gone, to which I sheepishly said I'd been too busy to sprout for him.

Most of my time was spent at this cafe, aptly named Sailors Bar. Every tanned, wrinkly faced sailor was there, eating the cheapest thing on the menu, sipping 1euro coffees and tap water to prolong their Internet connectivity. I wholly joined in, becoming friends with the regulars who all knew my story, asking me how I was going and when I was leaving. Truth be told I was doing great, although partially stuck in the Canaries while a set of solar panels took their sweet time in arriving from Germany. The Spanish postal system *Correos* was an absolute nightmare, these panels of considerable value simply vanishing somewhere between Madrid and Gran Canaria. While the downtime and low cost nightly inside the marina gave me time to plan and work remotely, I was again edging into another seasonal conundrum. My crossing of the Atlantic needed to happen soon, being already months out of the traditional crossing period before Christmas - it was now coming into March.

While prolonging a coffee that was now beyond cold, a Texan walked up and asked if he could share my table. He introduced himself as Mohammad, but he looked more like a Bryan to me. Unable to contain my curiosity I struck up a conversation, which resulted in an invitation aboard his boat for dinner that night. Asking where in the marina he was located, he pointed over to the commercial shipping dock. Astonishingly, Mohammad owned a 30 metre cargo ship and lived aboard with two cars and a Ducati, which could be lifted ashore with the cargo crane. Later that night, I briskly walked down to the commercial dock and found his boat, which sure enough, was a beaten up old rusty cargo ship with a torn U.S flag, lightly flapping off the pilothouse roof. Mohammad proudly invited me onboard and took me on a tour below decks, which sure enough contained two cars, a Ducati, thousands of cans of tomatoes, various dry stores, and several boxed fridges. Mohammad sailed the boat with just one other person, whom he'd find a week or so before making a passage. Otherwise, he lived onboard alone, maintaining all the various systems, engines, generators and ancillary equipment without help. The authorities never took kindly to him, repeatedly getting caught up in bureaucracy with every entry, his record being 18 months in Belgium where his boat was locked to the wharf. Purchased in Norway, the boat had spent its life collecting seaweed for the Japanese seafood market, giving the entire vessel a permanent odour.

We went up into the galley and began making pasta from scratch, a stainless steel pasta machine permanently bolted to the bench. Mohammad told me of his plans to sail to India, to convert the cargo ship to sail, so he could do Atlantic crossings at virtually no cost (the boat cost 400eurs a day in diesel). Everything Mohammad said sounded downright crazy, but he always had something to back his stories up, soon pulling architecturally drafted plans out of his cabinet to show me. The same cabinet contained several hand guns which he unloaded before handing to me. They were surprisingly heavy and beautifully crafted, objects which could be fetishised like expensive watches, brass compasses and other pieces of alluring craftsmanship. Having to go to the toilet, I peed off the high decks of the cargo ship and returned to the galley, which now had an enormous bag of Moroccan marijuana sitting on it. The leaves were white with crystals, as he rolled a joint and crushed some of the crystalline buds into the mix. He then started regaling me with a story about Doberman dogs back at home, grabbing my arm with great strength out of nowhere as a means to illustrate their lockjaw, making me jump with fright. It was at this point when Mohammad was well into his joint that I made my exit. I thanked him for his hospitality, stories and tour of his ship, as I walked down the gangplank. My last image of Mohammad was of a wiry tanned Texan, sitting next to a glistening pasta machine with two handguns and a bag of weed on the table, looking a lot more like a Bryan.

CLOSER TO SATELLITES THAN LAND

In the end, over two months were spent in Gran Canaria, waiting on solar panels which took 7 weeks to be shipped from Hamburg to the islands, temporarily lost in the system. I spent my days going stir crazy, swimming, writing emails and meeting unusual people. Needing a spare portable GPS as a backup before embarking on my crossing, I began asking around the marina to see whether anyone had something I could buy second-hand. A few weeks before, I'd met a young German named Peter who was living on a 45ft ketch on the neighbouring pontoon. The owner of the ketch was about to fulfil a lifelong dream to sail across the Atlantic, voyaging with his son from Hamburg to complete an Atlantic loop. The father stood on the deck one morning smoking a cigarette and abruptly fell over on the forepeak and died of a heart attack. The family didn't know what to do with the boat, the son leaving in utter shock soon after. Out of distress, the son put Peter, who they'd only met a few weeks beforehand, in charge of the boat until they could overcome their loss. Peter didn't have much money, an avid ocean swimmer who spent every morning paddling 1km out to sea and back. But there was something off about Peter, a sense I could never put my finger on. One evening he told me he was in the Canaries avoiding the Police, for the attempted armed robbery of a bank in Austria - in all honesty I wouldn't have put it past him. The next day he mentioned he had a handheld GPS he could sell me for 40eurs. I made the questionable moral decision to buy it, knowing full well it was likely not his to sell. This was the second time I'd let my moral compass be swayed, the first in Portsmouth where I was quite certain the fishermen at the pub were not selling me used personal goods out of the kindness of their hearts.

Spending a day mounting the solar panels on the pushpit and wiring them into the battery bank, I soon began looking at the weather forecast in earnest, spotting a moderately good window coming up for departure. The following two days were spent provisioning *Constellation* for our long journey across the Atlantic. My estimated crossing time was 25-30 days if all went well, however I was provisioning for two months in case something went awry, while also planning ahead to keep myself fed in the Caribbean, where supermarkets were limited and expensive. The water tank in *Constellation* always pumped water of questionable quality, so I only ever used the tank for cooking. As such, this also meant all other water had to be bought in bottles and stowed throughout my small ship. In the water aisle at the supermarket, I lifted 25x four litre bottles into my trolley, basing my calculations on two litres a day of pure drinking water. The unexpected benefit of all these bottles was that I couldn't foul my tank and end up stranded without drinking water - the worst thing I could do is puncture one or two bottles. Because *Constellation* was so tiny, I was also able to evenly distribute the weight throughout the hull and keep her balanced. Walking out of the supermarket I hailed a taxi to help me carry everything back to the boat, and spent the entire afternoon packing *Constellation* tight, jamming rice, potatoes and eggs into every available crevice. Potatoes could be stored for a long time if kept in the dark, while I coated the eggs in vaseline as a means of preservation. With any luck, if I turned the eggs upside down every week, I figured I would easily be able to make them last the voyage without being refrigerated. Psychologically it was taxing to plan two months in advance, knowing full-well the ramifications if things were forgotten. I would lay awake at night, my mind ticking over, pondering and pondering what I was forgetting - just imagine for a moment that you have to plan the next two months and you have absolutely no access to anything during that period if you mess it up: it's actually really terrifying!

When you loiter around a place long enough, people eventually become familiar faces on the street. You start remembering the names of the little French kids playing on the dock, notice the recent German ship has a new crew, and people start asking you about your missing shipment or finally inquire as to what your name is. Two weeks ago I met Carl at the infamous Sailors Bar, after subconsciously noticing we were both out here alone. There must be an unspoken rule, in that there is a period of time in waiting before one makes the effort to strike up a conversation. Because sailing is so transient, sometimes it's almost a fruitless exercise making any kind of connection with someone, because it's highly likely they will be gone the next day, never to be seen again. Nevertheless I was glad to have met Carl, a singlehander doing a delivery of his former yacht to the new owner in Guadeloupe. We spoke casually on and off, but I recognised there was something more to him, and I was unusually disappointed to see him off. It was really an unexpectedly intense experience, as I stood on the pontoon watching him sail out through the breakwater, as I felt a deep pang in my heart for his undertaking. Not a feeling of fear for his safety, but really just a level of understanding in what he was doing, and even a glimpse of what was to come for myself in the next few days. There was such a quietness in the air, and even an early onset feeling of solitude to his departure; this act of a lone person sitting there in the cockpit of their boat, in something so small, about to voyage across such a great expanse of 'nothingness'. I could sense his nervousness as I pushed his bow off the pontoon, even though he was highly experienced. I watched him sail out without glancing back, departing without spectacle, as people nosily watched from the cockpits of their boats with disinterested looks. It was just another boat leaving the marina with an unknown destination, just like they do every other day.

Rarely does one meet people who speak not of

theories, ideas or bolstered stories, but someone who exudes the purity of their experience. These are the most exceptional people you can ever hope to meet, and if detected, one must politely and intelligently spend as much time as one can with them. These are the people you watch and listen to, leaving your own ego at the door. They often have the social intelligence to detect who you are and what you are about, because they have lived a life of experience and this experience has taught them to acutely observe. In feeling this, it becomes prudent to keep one's own babbling talk to an absolute minimum: keep quiet, question with intellect, listen and watch. As I sailed, every manner of person wanted to offer an opinion or a piece of advice and my ability to quickly decide who was worth listening to became sharper and sharper.

Carl spent ten years sailing around the world with his wife and three children, surviving by his own wit and hard work, oftentimes providing for his family with only fish and island fruits. He is the type of person that no matter what you did to him; whether you dropped him in the desert, popped him on a rickety raft in the Atlantic, or threw him in jail, he would survive and carry on with little fuss. I guess in a sense, this is one of the reasons I'm out here myself; to build the kind of character that is strong, experiential and effortless, my small attempt to wash away those illusions we've encased ourselves in, whether we constructed them on our own, or had them thrust upon us by others.

I woke up on the day of my departure with nothing

left to do. There often comes a point in preparation on a boat when you really know it's time to leave - when everything is done and the only thing left is to actually set sail. It's always such a build up in one's head: psychologically preparing, letting your friends know that you really are leaving, calling your parents, triple checking your notes and lists. However, one day it all just stops, a sense of calm overtakes all the madness of managing the small details of living and preparation, and nothing is left but the task at hand - the thing all this busy-ness was actually for. It feels ceremonious in one's head, as if it's a big achievement to be ready for departure, but as you wake up and poke your head out the door, the realisation soon dawns upon you that departure day is actually just like any other day. The sun shines, the wind blows and the day is uncaring about your achievements or what you're about to do. At first it's a bit disappointing, but there is also a sense of excitement around just being able to get on with the job ahead: sail with the wind at your back until you see land again, however long it takes - and don't die.

My neighbour Paul was already at work, so another dock neighbour offered to take a photo of my departure and email it to me. He pushed the bow of *Constellation* off the dock and I reversed into the fuel dock to top off my tanks - it would be the last time I saw a familiar face. The Spanish fuel attendant asked where I was going and I responded *'the Caribbean'*. He looked at me and my small boat with an eye of adventure, having no doubt seen countless young men in small boats at his dock before. After paying my bill he handed me two t-shirts with the name of the fuel dock on them for good luck - one yellow, one blue. Ten years on, I still have these t-shirts tucked away, musty and faded - I mostly use them when cutting firewood now, but I've never forgotten who gave them to me and the good luck they brought.

It was late morning, the tanks were full and our departure was imminent. Motoring out of the breakwater, my friend snapped a few photos of me waving triumphantly from the end of the wall, as I raised the mainsail and jib, sailing slowly down the eastern side of Gran Canaria in a light northerly. Catedral de Santa Ana, San Jose, San Cristobal Campus and other Canarian landmarks slowly passed by. By late afternoon I popped underneath the island as the wind became more favourable for my western passage. I set my self-steering to 210 degrees on the compass, a heading I seemed to have been sticking to virtually since leaving Holland. If one is ever in Europe and needing to get to Australia in some kind of post-apocalyptic event, my recommendation is to point to 210 degrees and sail until you hit the Americas, make your way to the Pacific however you wish, then just keep going on the same heading until you hit the Land Down Under and someone gives you a Vegemite sandwich. This was my strategy anyway.

As dusk began its inevitable descent upon the horizon, I became anxious about what lay ahead. With every long passage, the first night was always terrifying - sleep is troubled and one's nerves are on high alert. In British small boat lore, to which I was aptly connected, there is a saying which goes *'Fear by day; terror by night'*, summing things up rather perfectly. It usually took 2-3 days offshore for me to become comfortable with the rhythm, risk and environment. Feeling seasick, night felt endless as I lay in my bunk listening to all the familiar sounds of *Constellation*, stretching and flexing with the unending movement of the ocean. Anticipating queasiness, I chewed on the raw ginger I had bought for this very occasion. As I nibbled away I wondered if the makeup of ginger had anything to do with alleviating my sickness, or whether it was just such a strong flavour that I became distracted from feeling sorry for myself.

Thankfully my first 24 hours were reasonably nice sailing, giving me time to acclimatise before a gruelling three days of unexpectedly miserable conditions. With a fairly unfavourable wind which was unusual for the season, along with a heavy cross-swell, *Constellation* and I were ceaselessly battered as we sailed off-course in an attempt to soften the ride. On the third night out at 4am, *Constellation* sailed out of control in a heavy squall with too much jib up. With my rusty pliers, I'd again be up on the foredeck, riding *Constellation* like a horse, both legs over the bow, my groin jammed into the forestay. *Constellation* bucked like a Brumby, the entire bow taking me underwater as I held onto the rails for dear life, pliers stuck between my teeth to free up both hands for holding on. As *Constellation* resurfaced and ejected what felt like a swimming pool worth of water overboard, I would quickly undo as many clips as I could before holding back on as we went back underwater. After what felt like an eternity, the jib was off and we had slowed down enough for everything to feel a little more controlled. I changed the sail out for something smaller, retreating into the cabin as fast as I could, soaked and shaking.

The interior of *Constellation* was a mess, books and potatoes had flown everywhere - I rescued *Flaubert* who had somehow managed to fly right out of the cabin and into the cockpit. At this point, I was really angry. Not because *Madame Bovary* was trying to jump overboard, but because this wasn't how it was supposed to be. This was *trade wind sailing*. I was *supposed* to be dawdling downwind without a care in the world, reading books and enjoying the stars! The anticipation of leaving and all the work up to this point wasn't working out exactly as I had planned, which, as usual, was a recipe for endless disappointment. This pattern of thinking - of expecting things to be a certain way - was an ongoing lesson which *Constellation* and the elements taught me. In hindsight, if I were to try and analyse things, its origin was perhaps intermingled with my grappling for control - of trying to anticipate my experience and control it. By the third day I'd come to terms with things and let it all go: we would sail as we would sail, come what may.

By the middle of the Atlantic, we'd come to a point where we were closer to orbiting satellites than we were to land. I was in awe of this fact, staring at my chart, which was spread out virtually from the port side of *Constellation's* interior to the starboard side. This was either a testament to how large the chart was (and how large the Atlantic was), or a testament to how small

Constellation was. It was a bit of both I guess. Falling into a strange kind of mid-Atlantic depressive malaise, I lay on the cabin sole of the boat, trying to find a position of least movement - the lower I was in *Constellation's* centre of gravity, the less we rolled. Laying on the floor, I wanted to cry so badly, the never-ending movement and loneliness suddenly all hitting me at once. Over and over in my mind I was lamenting the stupidity of it all, my decisions, the things I'd given up, the relationships I'd severed. All for this... rolling around and miserable, completely alone, quite literally in the middle of the ocean, feeling tired and sorry for myself. I thought about British yachtswoman Ellen McArthur who often had quite dramatic crying moments on camera as she battled through the southern ocean alone. Thinking of her I knuckled up and realised how easy this was in comparison. Or was it? It's hard to make comparisons of 'hardness', everyone's journey is their own, their experience entirely relative and subjective.

Carrying a video camera onboard, I would take it out of its bag and try to describe how I was feeling and what was going on. The moments of pure bliss which I experienced along the passage were rarely recorded: I used the camera as a person to complain to, more often than not. Whenever my mood was low, the conditions were hard, or there was something to complain about, the video camera came out, the lens staring back at me like a nodding therapist. Jack, who had been working on the film about my voyage, gave me a jar full of hand written questions, as a means to jolt something meaningful in these daily talks to myself. Each day I would pull out a question, some being ridiculous, others being philosophical in nature. One read '*Do you think children will one day sing a song in school about your voyages?*' I laughed at the idea that this voyage or perhaps anything I did would amount to much at all in the grand scheme of things. My ego was depleted out here, the *force majeure* of my surroundings humbled any sense of grandeur I had in this undertaking. Each day I just felt happy to be alive. As I lay my head on my pillow each night, I would wonder if I was going to wake up or be struck by disaster and bad luck while I dreamt.

During those moments of almost spiritual awakening, I would spend hours staring into the horizon, meditatively standing in the cockpit, my hands held together behind my back, simply balancing with the motion of *Constellation* as we surfed and rolled west towards an almost mythical destination: The Caribbean. Each day was full of simple joys, waking up many times throughout the night to check on *Constellation*, our bearing, the rig, marvelling momentarily at the stars, scanning the horizon for any sign of an impending squall. Ducking back to bed, I would again ponder whether I would wake up, the never-ending fear of collision or instantaneous sinking never leaving my mind. Every morning I would wake to a luminous sunrise and spend several hours in the cockpit drinking coffee, simply marvelling. By 9am it was too hot to be outside and I retreated into the cabin to read until sunset. Between chapters of great books, *Madame Bovary* finally dried her pages enough to be read, I would maintain our course, trim sails and tweak the windvane.

Whether it was night or day became utterly irrelevant. The world became timeless once again. I slept when I was tired, worked the boat or read when I was awake, ate food, and meditated on the horizon. This was the simple existence of my daily, hourly life. *Constellation* and I had created our own tiny floating universe, we lived at the mercy of everything around us, navigating our way west. My job and our goal was extremely simple: we just had to keep moving, that was all. This existence was unlike any other existence I had ever experienced - utter simplicity permeating everything, as my brain tried to unravel itself from an existence of battling the many complexities and externalities found in a *'normal'* life.

Life on land was full of details and contradictions - one's attention is under incessant attack. Out here, my emotions, my ingrained habits and inconsistencies were constantly bumping up against the simple harmony of nature. Each day would contain moments of bliss where I would let everything go and simply be at peace with everything, at last. These moments remained elusive, arising as they pleased, unable to harness or schedule their arrival. I felt as though my psyche was undergoing a transformation - perhaps an old self kicking and screaming to hold onto past thoughts, as if one side of my brain were in a great battle with the other side, or the 'id' (ego). Every moment was different, the sea never looked the same, *Constellation* never moved the same way twice and the wind never sung the same tune. Amongst all this solitude, all this fear and all this movement, an unraveling happened as I stared at the night sky and realised my size in the universe. Instead of a pending terror in my place within it all, a tremendous gratitude at how wonderful it was to be so free and alive poured out of me. Out of my existential realisation of how small, pointless and insignificant I was, came an extraordinary and lasting joy - a simple and acute joy of existence, which even today I can take solace in during my most trying moments.

CARIBBEAN LANDFALL

Surveying spiritual and mental shifts which lasted minutes or days, my journal entries became an outpouring of oddness, as if much of what I was experiencing couldn't actually be documented or saved. As such, what could be written down seemed eternally restless, mirroring a seemingly constant state of dissatisfaction.

"Feeling a little stir crazy and impatient now, with still at least 12 or more days to go, assuming the wind stays as-is. I'm thinking way too much... It's impossible to stop all this mental junk coming into one's head and invading all your thoughts. On land you can distract yourself with a myriad of things. Here there is nothing, literally, nothing! It's a fight in your own mental battle arena, completely of your own making in every way. Except *I* (or is it the id?) always lose...! Days, nights and weeks are all one. Or none. I don't know anymore. Time has lost all meaning, space has lost all sense. I ate jelly beans for breakfast."

On day 24, I woke with a jump thinking *Constellation* was on fire, a predicament no sailor ever wishes to encounter. The thought of one's floating universe quite literally burning down around their feet was roughly on par with the fear of falling overboard while peeing, watching *Constellation* sail under autopilot into the horizon. These two terrors, along with a suite of others including every manner of collision (whale, shipping container, tanker) were daily considerations. Asleep, I dreamt that the electrical system was short-circuiting, sending *Constellation* up in flames. I woke up startled and confused, but the sound of the electrical system short circuiting didn't stop, as I reeled around wondering what was going on. To my relief and amusement, a flying fish had flown through the forward hatch, beating its wings on the cabin floor in escape.

While my crossing wasn't as smooth as it could have been because of my lateness in the season, overall it wasn't as bad as it could have been either. The weather patterns did seem less consistent from my reading and reports from other sailors, however with three days to go, I was feeling confident. Before long, three days became 24 hours, and I started to realise I'd very nearly achieved something quite impressive. And then I had. My journal read:

"Wow, it's done. I arrived at 14:10 in Port St Charles. I docked on the fuel berth and stood on land. It was an incredibly odd feeling. I had to see Customs,

Immigration and Health before being allowed back on my boat... I went out and anchored in Six Mans Bay. The water is warm, there are kids playing on the beach, the sand is white and I just can't believe it. How beautiful; what an extraordinary and great day."

After several years in Europe, arriving in the Caribbean was both a culture-shock and a shock of landscape. Everyone was *cool*. I mean, really cool. The graffiti covered buses played hip hop and sported racing car spoilers, there was music everywhere and generally the people seemed less inhibited and tremendously friendly. Amongst pristine white beaches, *Constellation* lay anchored in crystal clear water out the front of the Bridgetown yacht club. The chief of the immigration department insisted that the best way to enjoy Barbados was to drink plenty of Rum, meet a local girl and party as much as possible. He said you only live once. Diving overboard into the warm water, I swam down on the anchor, dug in the pearl white sand, looking back up at *Constellation* from the seabed. The fact we were here was simply unbelievable, the years of preparation and constant pushing to cross the Atlantic had actually created this success. The dogged and tireless desire to just *keep moving* really did yield results, to my own constantly second-guessing astonishment.

Barbados was a strategic stopover, as I had decided to sail to New York to escape the hurricane season and work out my next move, both financially and physically. The Panama Canal was my only route through to the Pacific, and from my research it seemed that the transit would be in excess of $2000 US dollars. This was in addition to the difficulty of taking such a small and slow boat through the locks, not to mention I had less than $500 left to my name. With family and the offer of a free berth in New York at a marina on Long Island, the opportunity to sit still for a while and reassess how I was going to keep moving was a valuable one. The passage to New York was almost as far as the Atlantic, and perhaps in some ways a more risky proposition. Barbados was the only place in the Caribbean with a U.S embassy, so my stopover was to obtain a B1/B2 visa so I could legally enter the U.S aboard *Constellation*.

The lateness of my arrival into the leeward islands meant I didn't have a tremendous amount of time to enjoy the fruits of all this voyaging because the hurricane season was rapidly approaching. On the second day I was lined up at the U.S embassy, ticket number 61 in hand. By midday I spoke to a U.S official about the requirements for the visa I needed: proof of employment and a bank statement displaying sufficient funds. My heart began to pound before it promptly sunk at the news. The last time I'd had a real job was literally years before and my bank statement showed less than a thousand dollars. I walked back into town, contemplating how to resolve this new hurdle. My walking meditation on how to get around this curly problem turned more into the following consideration: All forms of bureaucracy demand one thing - a response which meets their limited criteria without complexity. Or, in simple terms, it is best to tell such institutions what they wish to hear, rather than the more common reality that things are almost always more complex.

Night fell on *Constellation* as we bobbed lightly in the Caribbean breeze. The engine was running so I could run my laptop without destroying the battery and I began to creatively generate a suite of documents '*proving*' my suitability to enter mainland U.S. By midnight I had a letter of employment explaining that I was actually on holiday, along with a bank statement which painted a brighter picture than reality. Back in line the next morning at 7.30am, I sweated nervously under the air conditioner, looking down at my ticket number, amused to see the number 42, the number representing the meaning of life in *The Hitchhiker's Guide to the Galaxy*. The woman at the desk glanced at my forged documents with a less than discerning eye, which I had just printed off at a tobacco shop for 15 cents. She looked back at me without expression and sent me to the interview room, where lay the true jury of bureaucrats. The interviewer plainly asked me what I was doing and why I needed the visa. I answered truthfully as he glanced at my documents and listened with a surprising look of intent. Looking back up at me, he asked which of the large cruise ship companies I was working for, assuming my mention of the word 'boat' in several sentences previously meant something significantly larger than the bathtub I had sailed in on. Taking a large breath, I told my story with honesty, as the interviewer stared down at the paperwork without showing any emotion or looking up, my regaling of a perilous journey across the Atlantic not even producing a brief moment of eye contact. After finishing the short version of a much longer story about sailing and adventure and the universe and solitude and beauty, the interviewer took my passport and said the visa would be stamped and sent via courier to Saint Lucia within 5 working days. As I possessed dual citizenship, I was able to leave one of my passports with the embassy and exit Barbados on my second passport, bound for Saint Lucia, allowing me to move onto the next island in the leeward chain without waiting for 5 days for the embassy to process my visa.

The ongoing financial stress climaxed as I began my exit out of Barbados with customs requesting a $100USD exit fee to receive the exit paperwork required to enter the next country. The haphazard system of managing the state and whereabouts of small boat sailors is that with every entry into a new country, paperwork displaying dates of exit from the previous country are handed over. Upon entering the new country, if the time between exit and entry is unusually exorbitant (for example, it's taken you two months to sail a very short passage), the entering country may notice this discrepancy, search your boat more thoroughly and put you through a lot of questioning. The space on passage between countries is almost 'stateless', where one exists almost without nationality and beyond borders, culture or control. I loved thinking about this, thinking of it as a true *'terra nullius'*. As a form of nearly pointless protest, I explained *ad hominem* to the customs official that I literally didn't have $100 to give him. He looked at me quizzically and simply said I couldn't leave. With time instead of money on my hands,

I petitioned the clearance fee without much success and decided to sit down until the officials became bored with me. Overlooking *Constellation* in the small office, I sat for 4.5 hours, being offered cake and coffee throughout the day, as if my tiny protest brought a kind of testing respect. The office hours ended at 4pm, the clock nearing day's end as I sat steadfast. At 4pm the customs master came over with my stamped paperwork and wished me a safe voyage. Shaking his hand, I glanced down at the paperwork and noticed the ship name as '*Constatution*' shrugging at the discrepancy as we sailed off the dock and into the setting sun for Saint Lucia. The handful of days on land soon meant a tired sense of seasickness, the swift pace of the Caribbean wind causing a choppy trade swell. Munching on a stick of ginger I had bought in anticipation of again feeling ill, I waved half-heartedly at passengers on a huge cruise ship headed back across the Atlantic.

My friend Jack from Germany who was working on the documentary of my trip had booked flights to Saint Lucia, timing his arrival based on my positions across the Atlantic, miraculously landing right as I sailed into Rodney Bay - his knack for timing flights was uncanny. Seeing Jack after feeling a pang of loneliness in Barbados was a great joy, again highlighting how self-contained and happy I felt mid-ocean, yet how lonely and existential I felt amongst people on land. I often wonder how many people in the world have felt such a deep loneliness without knowing the true and unexpected remedy was actually genuine aloneness in nature - rather than the more common self-prescribed act of surrounding oneself with friends and busyness.

Anchored inside the lagoon I was able to catch a weak and drifting WIFI signal to receive email. One email indicated my passport had arrived at the DHL office in Castries and a second email arrived with a bill from the people subletting my apartment in Germany for 1200 euros in electricity from previous tenants who had skipped out. I was fuming. In my rush to leave Berlin, I had left my apartment in my name and sublet it to my ex-girlfriend. She then sublet it to someone else, and then they sublet it to someone else - on and on, before I had no idea who was in the apartment at all. My mistake was leaving all the utilities and associated things in my name.

Jack and I drank a bottle of Barbados rum stashed in the bilge and dragged our hands through the water at night, watching immense bioluminescence create a trail behind our hands in the water. The next morning I emailed my dad asking him if I could borrow money to pay the electricity bill, the first and only time I had asked to borrow money on the voyage from my parents. With the money angrily transferred to the power company at an Internet kiosk in Castries, we picked up my passport from the DHL office and Jack proceeded to take some street B-roll shots of Castries for the film.

Having felt incessantly harassed in Rodney Bay, our guard was up as a man roughly my age approached, a tiger tattooed on the top of his hand, wearing dark sunglasses, a bandanna and a NYC badged baseball cap.

Preparing to say '*no no no we don't want to buy anything*', he proceeded to redirect his interest in the camera, wondering what we were doing and whether we were a real film crew. With hesitation, we explained what we were doing, before he decided to take us on an incredibly surreal, narrated whirlwind tour of the backside of Castries. Exceptionally quick witted, our new found friend was a musician, producer and hip hop singer who wove a story so intricate and full of flow it was impossible not to be utterly mesmerised. We couldn't work out if we were being taken on a ride which wasn't going to end well, or whether we had lucked-into an incredible human experience. Unable to say no to anything, we simply followed as we were introduced to his aunt selling Guyanian gold, his rasta friend selling *everything* and a man owning a bizarre medicinal store, simply called *The French Shop*, which appeared to sell magic powders, tinctures and ancient tins of secret crushed herbs. Tiny glass bottles with labels which looked freshly printed but unchanged since the 1950's crowded the shelves, entire walls full of aerosols containing love potions and spray-on good luck. In a bizarre twist, our unexpected tour guide took a political bent as we visited the Saint Lucia cultural centre, where a recent Taiwanese donation had been accepted by the government to help fund local culture works, which had mysteriously disappeared. As a means of political prodding, we stood at the front door, with Jack filming as two officials swiftly arrived by our side, questioning our presence. Without hesitation, our prankstering guide pointed to us as being a BBC film crew doing a piece of investigative journalism on international monetary gifts among Caribbean nations. Gob-smacked, Jack and I tried to keep a straight face, nodding with agreement and disbelief. The officials asked for our identification, which was quickly rebuffed by our guide in exclamation that we were under a signed contract for privacy reasons to protect our rights and identities as journalists. Swift, effortless talking with an almost rap-poetry sensibility saved our prank as we evaded further questions and retreated into the busyness of the town to eat fried chicken.

The following day we set sail, Jack staying onboard until Antigua where his short stay would end. With an unexpected headwind, we set anchor in Portsmouth, the second largest town in Dominica on the Indian river. Without any customs facilities, we snuck ashore for a few hours, searching for avocados before departing the next day. As we walked through town, there was a distinct feeling that we were not welcome. Lean, naturally athletic men with bandannas sat on car bonnets and watched us walk past in silence. It was eerie and threatening and I was glad to be back onboard unscathed - and with a bag of unripe avocados under my arm. We continued sailing the next day, passing Pigeon Island, former home of the French pirate *François le Clerc*, the first pirate to have actually had a peg leg, aptly named *Pata de Palo* (stick leg) by the Spanish. François had also sailed from the Canary Islands, where he had looted and set the island of La Palma on fire, which is exactly what I had felt like doing to Gran Canaria after waiting two months for *DHL* to deliver equipment I couldn't leave without. We passed a stone lighthouse perched high on a mountainous hill, where I felt for a brief moment like I was back in Brittany, France, navigating a tricky tidal race under a cold stiff breeze, the avocados rolling around on the cabin floor, hard as rocks.

The breeze turned favourable and we sped into English Harbour, Antigua, towards a stunning vista, a full moon to starboard and a setting sun. The natural harbour was fenced with mangroves and the architectural stone building charms of England. One's charged imagination could almost smell the hot tar and see sails being cut through the open loft doors - the glisten of varnished yachts catching remnants of the orange sun. Waking up the next morning to the sound of roosters, lush green flora, a polished yacht from Bristol to port and the Admirals Inn to starboard, Jack scurried ashore to catch his plane back to Berlin. I remained, pondering with some disappointment how I would soon be leaving all of this, bound for New York.

Later that afternoon, a girl swam over, asking if she could come aboard - 'sure' I said, as she pulled her topless self up into the cockpit. While I sat stunned and distracted, she asked if she could crew with me and sail to wherever I was going. Looking at *Constellation* with a slight feeling of dismay that she wasn't twice the size and more capable of sailing long distances with crew, I explained my ambition to sail solo, politely declining the opportunity with an aura of disappointment. Rebuffed, the girl whose name and image I quickly scrubbed from mind for the purposes of self-preservation, performed a perfect dive from the bow and swam ashore. Still affected by my first and only girlfriend who I'd left to go on this voyage, I was uptight and nervous around women, completely unable to read any signals or even display any interest.

Lord Nelson of the British Royal Navy was said to wake up every morning and have six buckets of water thrown over him for his daily hygiene routine. This was to be followed by a quart of goat's milk while bellowing loud complaints of mosquitos from the previous night, after which he would exclaim '*damn this infernal hole*' so loudly that the entire harbour could hear. I hadn't had a fresh water shower for the last eight weeks and rather adored this infernal hole, but every day I stayed meant increased hurricane danger going forward on my passage north. The voyage north to New York City was 1552 nautical miles across highly variable latitudes of differing wind angles and conditions. The infamous Horse Latitudes. My Atlantic crossing was just under twice the distance, but set in much more stable, consistent weather patterns. As was often the case, it was my naivete regarding what was to come which protected me from not going at all. At the chandlery in English Harbour, I read passage charts and books on the leg to Bermuda without buying anything, asking anyone who would talk to me about the passage to impart knowledge on what to expect or how to manage the Gulf Stream. One skipper asked me what my intended route was, to which I exclaimed '*a straight line to New York City*', whereby he looked at me quizzically, simply suggesting I leave soon, as if he didn't want to get too involved with a possible lunatic. This seemed to be a somewhat common sentiment.

Drinking tea aboard a small, green Cornish trader captained by a man named Peter who had sailed her across the Atlantic in 1989 and never left, I gleaned what knowledge I could over the crackling background radio of the BBC, which was broadcasting a cricket match. That same afternoon I provisioned for a voyage I expected to take 12-16 days with ramen and extra bottles of water from Antigua's closest thing to a supermarket, an expensive and small general store. The following morning I attempted to pull up the anchor for my departure, only to find it stuck, yet another sign I was searching for not to leave. Diving down, I found the anchor wrapped around a piece of chain left on the seabed, cut away from another yacht or carelessly dropped. During the process of untangling it all, I noticed it was a reasonable length of 12mm stainless anchor chain, which I ended up hauling on deck and salvaging for future use.

NEW YORK

Pulling the anchor up in Antigua was emotionally distressing. Hand over hand I pulled from the bow until the anchor was released and *Constellation* began to drift in the small harbour. It is at this moment that one is completely free of land, untethered from the comfort and security of solid earth, thrown back out into the unpredictable and watery unknown. In total I'd spent just under a month in the leeward islands of the Caribbean after my Atlantic crossing. I hadn't planned to stay for such a short period, but due to delays in the Canary Islands, I was now out of time. Put simply, I needed proper time to rest, explore and decompress from the Atlantic crossing - this departure was feeling rushed, unplanned and stressful. I sailed slowly under jib past a catamaran full of Frenchman who asked where I was headed: New York City I yelled. They clapped and cheered as I bowed, feeling rejuvenated by their encouragement and enthusiasm. A Venezuelan tanker passed a little too close for my liking a mile out, a quick reminder of the constant hazards while underway. Shortly after, I glanced down in confusion at the seemingly shallow water, pouncing on the helm to redirect course, expecting to ground on a reef. Checking my depth sounder and chart, I was relieved to note it was simply water of such clarity it appeared only feet deep. In just the last hour my emotions had run the full gamut. With enough breeze to hold the windvane on course, I retreated to my bunk for some reprieve.

By 2am on the second morning, we sailed through a tropical wave, a system which often becomes a hurricane when conditions are more favourable, as they are later in the season. For now, the system blew in excess of 40kts, lasting a full 3 hours before dropping us off into a calm, surrounded by an uncomfortable sea state - quickly followed by a squall for good measure. As the sun rose, we began to make good pace, the kettle boiling for coffee on the alcohol stove.

The days passed with inconsistency and sleeplessness. Normally I would comfort-eat my way through lack of sleep and the inability to relax, but my stores were dry. With 20 packets of ramen noodles, plain pasta, rice, four bags of flour, six packets of cookies and a bottle of chilli sauce, the pickings were slim. I still had my emergency rations from the Canary Islands, which were packets of Gofio, a Canarian cuisine I had read about which was used by a mad pair of twins from France who sailed across the Atlantic in a homemade outrigger, navigating with only a compass and their memory of the stars. They survived purely on water and Gofio, which can only be described as a fine flour which is mixed with milk or water, having both the taste and consistency of wallpaper paste. So, while it was unlikely I was going to die of starvation, it was quite clear I would not be delving into my Gofio stores in a bid to seek comfort from the elements.

On the sixth day, I reached an emotional zenith, feeling for the first time on the voyage so far, and perhaps in my life, that I did not wish to be doing anything else. For this feeling to arise, I had sailed for 250 days across 5500 nautical miles of ocean, finally experiencing a sense of *'enough'*. What was here, what was now, was at long last wholly complete and satisfying. In a sense, it was just this moment that I had actually come here for. It was not because I had a tremendous interest in sailing per se (although my love for sailing blossomed) - really, sailing was just the vessel taking me towards a state of mind. I was driven by a tremendous desire to test myself and find a sense of peace within it. In the *'nothingness'* which surrounded me, I discovered a richness unlike anything I had felt before, finally allowing the feeling to wash over me in full understanding that what I was feeling was temporal, yet divine.

By the eighth day, we were at 27 degrees north, in alignment with the latitude of the Canary Islands. As a little celebration, I poured some milk into a bowl and mixed it with Gofio, thinking back to my days in Gran Canaria, dreaming of checking my email and eating a cheese toasted sandwich at the Sailors Bar. By mid-morning, torrential rain screamed down from the low-lying clouds, reducing visibility to just a few hundred metres. In doing so, the rain created the most incredible sound against the sea, producing more water from the heavens than I have ever seen in my life. I jumped outside with a bar of soap, having an impromptu shower, filling bucket after bucket from the scuppers or dripping mainsail boom. The rain was cold, as I shivered on the foredeck waiting for the sun to dry me out. As I waited, a great sign of biblical proportions appeared right before my eyes - with a light drizzle, the sun penetrated the grey clouds, creating an extraordinary rainbow which ventured right down the very port side of *Constellation*. In the heart of the Bermuda Triangle, we had seemingly become the pot of gold at the end of the rainbow.

I thought a lot about the ominous Bermuda Triangle, a place where planes and boats mysteriously disappeared for unknown reasons. Laying in my bunk, I could hear *Constellation* drifting over a thicket of seaweed, a telling sign of the Sargasso Sea. I'd heard stories of ships being becalmed amongst the seaweed for weeks, which I thought wasn't entirely out of the realm of possibility for me, since I only had 10 litres of diesel onboard. The Gofio stared at me from the shelf.

The natural elements within the borders of the triangle certainly gave credence to the mishaps, but not because they were overtly mysterious or other-worldly, but rather because the region was so environmentally unstable, primarily because of the Gulf Stream and nature of the latitudes. One evening while reading, I smelt woodsmoke, which, as one can imagine, was both unexpected and worrying: the fear of my boat burning down around me returned swiftly. Leaping on deck, I saw no signs of fire, only a sky burned with a kind red intensity I had never seen before, from horizon to horizon. For days after, the sunrises and sunsets were extraordinary, while the faint smell of smoke lingered. It was only after landfall that I would learn the smoke was blowing 600 miles offshore from huge peat moss fires on the east coast - left to burn, the fires could not physically be extinguished, as they smouldered underground, the carbon-rich partially decomposed soil slowly burning with little flame and significant smoke, a phenomenon which can last for years.

It wouldn't be a stretch to say that one can almost sail by ear alone, particularly when sailing solo, the voices of others replaced with the voice of the vessel. The boat creaks, the rigging stretches, the lines flex and the hull sings with every lap of water. A solo sailor develops an additional set of secret powers, akin to a second crewmate. Sleep can be interrupted by just minor variances in wind or direction, should the autopilot waver, the waves change shape or their velocity modify. Because of this extra sensory perception, it's exceptionally difficult to relax, because the brain is under constant stress to process this information 24 hours a day. So while there is a common conception that calms drive a sailor crazy, I often relished them because I could finally relax wholly. As a calm would descend, I would rejoice at the idea of a break from it all, the sea state quietening and the varying noises diminishing, often replaced by a slapping sail as we bobbed without wind. Followed by a calm, there typically comes a time of beautiful sailing, as the wind begins to pick up, the sea playing catch-up and remaining flat for a period. The keel cuts through the water like a hot knife through butter, the slapping sails cease and the quietude is stunning and sharp. Down below over a book, there is the swishing sound of water across the hull, a kind of symphonic meditation on hydrodynamics, providing a calm, idyllic space for reading. These joys are short lived - with every calm, there is a cycle one participates in, as the swell builds again, the wind changes slightly, *ad infinitum.*

By day 22 of a voyage I expected to be at most 16 days, I was fed up. The conditions seemed to change by the hour, the strange and ominous weather changing at a moment's notice. As the smoke lifted, the horizon re-filled with dark squall clouds, electrical activity firing in every direction, day and night. I'd read about the effect of being hit by lightning, boats ending up with a thousand tiny pin-holes, sinking almost instantly with tiny jets of water. I'd lay awake at night, anxiously watching the cabin top flicker, wondering at what moment I would be struck. I thought about those silly lightning grounders some people have on their cars, promptly fashioning one up myself by grounding the metal mast stays to the windvane paddle which was in the water, as some kind of vain attempt to quash my anxiety, channeling Benjamin Franklin's kite experiment.

As we crossed the Gulf Stream, the iridescent blue ocean became a murky blue-grey, the transition from Caribbean waters to northern waters happening before my eyes. Watching the GPS, our track immediately changed as the Gulf current picked us up and started hurtling us towards Boston. Before long, without enough wind to counter the strength of the current, I noticed our GPS track begin to go in a circle as we became firmly caught in an eddy. Without enough diesel to motor out of the cycle, we sat for three full days, going in a circle, unable to break free, the peace I had discovered weeks earlier shattered with anger and frustration at the futility of it all. The temperature began to plummet as I rummaged through my lockers for the clothes I'd kept myself warm with through autumnal Europe, donning a mouldy jacket and a pair of wet woollen socks. As I sat in the cockpit in misery, I noticed the faintest white sail on the horizon, the first sign I wasn't alone in some weeks. The Challenge 67 was as surprised as I was to hear a voice on the radio, completely unable to see me visually or on radar. Having sailed from the ice pack of Antarctica, they were headed to Boston, which is exactly where I was going, too, but not out of choice. We bantered for a while, discussed the weather, before losing signal, never seeing or hearing from them again.

Trash and debris from New York City began to float by, as I steered directly at a wedding balloon, attempting to pick it up with my boat hook. A peanut butter jar, a piece of wood which looked surprisingly like a pair of antlers and other unidentifiable floating objects passed at regular intervals. The eddy wouldn't let go of its grip, as we became caught in a solid southerly current, now going backwards, sailing at a speed of 3kts through the water, but actually going 1-2kts in the opposite direction. The current bumped us back into blue Caribbean waters, however I was unable to tell which side of the Gulf we were on - were we now going to have to cross it again, or were we on the other side? By day 25 a brisk wind picked up and at long last, as I trimmed as much sail as we could carry, we began to make headway towards New York city. Within 12 hours the wind backed and we became caught again in an eddy, now headed south east - our desired course was north west. With ten litres of diesel left, I decided to burn five litres in a vain attempt to break us free of the current. After hours of fiddling with the engine which refused to start, we made a little progress.

To my surprise and relief, I heard humans on the radio at a time when I most needed a distraction: a navy warship was performing live tests in my vicinity and the coast guard was warning of an exploded yacht off Rhode Island - soon after I could hear the banter of yachtsmen in the Bermuda race. Over VHF radio I spoke with some of the racers, warning them of the eddy I'd been stuck in, providing rough coordinates. I didn't realise at the time, however, that experienced sailors of this region use the eddy's to their advantage to make swift headway, better understanding their patterns than I could, while also being able to receive synopsis charts which display their strength and locations before departure. It's possible I had inadvertently provided up to the minute eddy routing information, which may have been an advantage to anyone listening at that time.

On day 27, I was lying in my bunk reading when the distinct sound of dolphin sonar reverberated around the hull. Climbing on deck, I was greeted with one of the most spectacular displays of nature ever experienced: the chart indicated our crossing the continental shelf, bringing hundreds and hundreds of dolphins diving across the horizon, the sun rising behind them in a scene of wonderment. The magic of it all was almost impossible to comprehend. After days of struggle and negativity, nature provided the most perfect uplift as I glanced at the GPS with only 118 nautical miles to go.

By late afternoon we lay hove-to, surrounded by fishing boats in a squall of considerable strength. Incredibly, I was experiencing some of the strongest winds of the entire voyage, as I lay down below wondering if something very bad was about to happen. Within half an hour we lay becalmed and I spoke to nearby fishermen on the radio who seemed as surprised as I was at the power of the passing squall. By 2am, six fishing boats were spaced equally across the horizon, appearing to slowly move as I approached at 3kts, creating a path for me into New Jersey. The emotion of seeing port entry lights on the horizon, the almost choreographed movement of other vessels to let me pass after 28 days at sea, was tremendous. While still pitch-black, visibility began to dramatically decrease, which before long left me in utter darkness, surrounded by a deep, dense fog.

The wind lightened to a standstill and I started the engine with only an hour or two of diesel left, ghosting along at 4kts in the famous Ambrose Channel. Buoys with audible gongs bobbed in the darkness, creating a terrible sense of eeriness. I could see no further than the end of the bow, listening intently to place myself correctly within the shipping channel, the sound of diesel engines emanating from the fog. A research vessel radioed me, calling for a *'small vessel moving at 3-4kts within the channel'*. Knowing full-well it was me, I replied in a panic, wondering if we were on a collision course. With professionalism the captain said he could see me on radar and was steering clear. I said I was a small sailboat under limited power after a month at sea making headway for New York. His response was one of congratulations and respect, the engines passing by and lifting my spirits. The fog began to lift slightly, a tugboat quickly followed by a commercial fishing vessel passed as I spotted the long beach of New Jersey, and I made way for Sandy Hook.

We had made it. I dropped anchor and a man named Phil paddled over almost immediately with a cold beer and a banana, exclaiming that I looked like I could do with something cold and healthy: this man knew the hardships of my arrival without even asking. The sense of relief and accomplishment as I sat in the cockpit was astronomical. I was in the U.S.A.

Borrowing Phil's dinghy, I rowed ashore to find

something to eat and proceed with customs and immigration paperwork. The technical details of how to actually enter into the U.S were not wholly clear from the people I had asked - or what was written in my varying guides. There seemed to be no official customs office at the marina, nor anyone who appeared to really care that I'd just turned up, unannounced from waters afar. Surprised at the lack of authority, I felt like I'd just snuck into one of the most notoriously security-conscious countries on the planet. I walked to the nearest town and found a diner.

Sitting at a bench seat at the diner, I ordered a Californian Deluxe hamburger with a side main of Caesar salad with extra chicken, three cups of coffee and a root beer. Everything felt surreal as I flipped through the New York Times, glancing at the tennis on the TV. For the first time on my entire trip, I felt a little chuffed at how far I'd come: I felt like I had accomplished something real, a sense I hadn't allowed myself to feel until now for whatever reason.

Walking back to *Constellation* with a full stomach, I stopped at a phone booth along the way to call the 1-800 number I'd gleaned from the Internet, which I was supposed to call to find out the specifics of the check-in procedure for the port of New Jersey. Instructed to visit Port Newark, I stopped at a bench seat just outside the marina to sit down, soak it all in and work out how to get to Newark: the U.S is a place which is inhospitable to those without a car and a cell phone.

A rotund man walked past with a dog, changing course for the same bench I was on, sitting down and saying hello. Only having spoken to two people since my arrival (Phil and the waitress), I decided to ask the man where Port Newark was. Instead of answering with some simple directions or even pointing, he interrogated me with an alarming number of questions in quick succession, which I answered nonchalantly, eager to regale my story of arriving just hours before. To my surprise, the man flat out refused to believe a word I had just said, accusing me of some kind of ruse! Of all the people on the planet to ask for directions, I had just asked an off-duty Special Customs Agent how to enter the country! He produced his ICE badge as evidence and asked to see my paperwork, which I carried everywhere. After a quick exchange of identification and boat papers, his tone changed and lightened, realising everything I'd just said was actually true, offering to drive me to Port Newark the following morning.

Back on *Constellation*, my brother who I hadn't seen for over two years took the speed-cat over from Manhattan. I picked him up off the jetty with a borrowed dinghy from another anchored yacht, the crew taking pity on my attempts to row my deflated Avon raft in a stiff breeze. On dropping the dinghy off, they slung over a bag of beer, pasta, fruit and a huge freshly cooked steak of striped bass. My brother, who had never been aboard *Constellation* got the grand tour - which can be taken all without leaving the cockpit. Norwegian friends in Spain would often note how handy a tiny sailboat was, because you could cook, navigate, helm and sleep, all without getting up!

The following morning, my friendly local customs agent picked me up in his enormous Ford truck, taking me to Port Newark via Buffalo Donut where we got coffee and donuts for the 10 minute drive to our destination. Entering the large commercial port, designed and setup for dealing with large commercial tanker crew, I was heartily introduced to the on duty officer, an old friend of my personal escort. They bantered and he told the story of our chance meeting to the entire office who laughed and joked, as my paperwork was scanned, signed, dated and stamped. Within 20 minutes my new friend dropped me off at the Newark train station where I ventured into Manhattan, exiting near the World Trade Centre. The quiet and insular life aboard my tiny boat was now well and truly over, and I entered the seemingly endless wave of foot traffic heading every which direction. Unable to cope, I soon retreated to the closest cafe I could without people, recuperating in the corner from human-overload, soon returning to *Constellation* where I slept for 14 hours.

While in the Caribbean, a New Yorker by the name of Tony had been in contact, helping me with weather and offering me any assistance he could while in New York. After leaving New Jersey, I headed to Sheepshead bay in Coney Island, a free anchorage just a short row to the subway and shops. Sailing past roller coasters, Tony arrived with a power boat to take some photos of us sailing, capturing moments in front of the Statue of Liberty and the Manhattan skyline. My engine was struggling along, before Tony offered to simply tow me wherever I needed to go, taking me at speed up to the 79th Street Boat basin where I met friends and family. The following day I navigated through Hell's Gate, the notorious tide pulling me along, zooming through the Gate at a steady 9kts, faster than the parallel NYC commuter traffic.

While sailing under the Brooklyn bridge, an extraordinary line-squall built, generating an ominous deep purple sky and brisk winds, further accelerating my exit into Long Island Sound, where Tony generously met me again, towing me into Stamford, where I stayed with him and his wife for two nights. On the first morning with Tony, he asked me after breakfast whether I needed any new clothes. Slightly perplexed, I said I was ok. He laughed and said *'Nick, I think you need some new pants'* - I looked down and realised I did look pretty disheveled. I'd become used to living alone in the elements, perhaps not equipped to be living in the modern world I'd so quickly found myself in. Tony could tell I was really broke. Part of the reason why I wasn't interested in clothes shopping was because I simply couldn't afford it - the following day we went shopping for new clothes. Tony asked if I liked a pair of jeans, the colour of a t-shirt, etc. I said yes, tried them on, and he grabbed a few of everything and paid for it all. I was humbled. He later took me shopping for food provisions - on the third day it was time for me to leave - Tony and his wife Eva handed me an envelope with $1000 in it. I nearly cried - it was so generous and I needed it so badly. Their support and kindness was unbelievable, and I humbly sailed towards Port Jefferson with a renewed energy.

By this point, *Constellation* was literally falling apart right around me. It's as if she had known to stay together and get me to this point, but now she had nothing left and was crumbling out of exhaustion. I understood - so was I. With a plume of white smoke en route to Duck Island, the engine spluttered and stopped, refusing to come back to life. We began drifting across the Sound, before a slight favourable breeze appeared from nowhere, propelling us to a safe anchorage where we stayed the night, staying up late with wrenches in my hand, attempting to work out the engine issue. Unable to resolve the problem, we patiently waited for the sea breeze to fill in the following day after lunch, proceeding under sail for the town of Greenport, where I had been offered a slip for summer. This opportunity was an act of grace from the marina manager, the father of a friend from university who had offered to help me out. This was a huge boon, providing time and space to work out what was next and how to proceed onwards: The Pacific Ocean beckoned, but this enormous continent stood in the way. The generosity of new friends in the U.S, from the very moment I landed in New Jersey, continued to shock and humble me. It was almost impossible to walk the dock in Greenport without someone wanting to talk to me, offer a helping hand or put me in touch with someone who might be able to help with any of the thousand issues *Constellation* now had.

It was summer now, as I slept aboard and used the

marina tea room as my office. Day in and day out I researched, emailed and thought about what was next and how to continue - the voyage never wavered and there was never any rest.

The snow arrived in New York, *Constellation's* deck covered as she lay hauled out at the Brewers Yacht Yard in Greenport, NY. Mike, the marina manager at Brewers took great care of me at a time of uncertainty in my voyage, my days spent working on the logistics of how to continue on to the Pacific. My arrival had sparked some local interest, the newspaper running a frontage article on my trip and arrival into Greenport, which piqued the interest of some generous individuals.

Walking around the yard one day, a rigger came over and mentioned there was a boat with some people looking for me. Intrigued, I went back to *Constellation* and met a family who had seen the article in the paper and wanted to help me by running a fundraising BBQ at their house. Without hesitation I said yes, the party being organised the following week to help raise funds for my idea of trucking *Constellation* across the U.S.A. Just a week later, my new friends put on a BBQ at their beautiful house in Greenport, inviting friends and family to come along to meet me and help support the trip west to the Pacific. With tremendous gratitude, a third of the monies required to truck *Constellation* was raised, as I excitedly announced I was going to bicycle across the country as *Constellation* sat rested on a trailer for the trip: This new addition never eventuated, the seasons didn't match up with the idea and the reality was I needed no further lunacy added to the project, but the drive and energy I had in New York from the successful crossing from Europe somehow gave a sense that I was invincible. The support, interest and energy surrounding the voyage was at an all time high, a sense that after all my toiling away and grinding to make it this far was somehow being recognised by others. It was a difficult time to describe, there existed an unexpected energy in my life which was attracting so much support I was overwhelmed - it was as if I had become somehow magnetic to opportunity. It was unexplainable but wonderful.

With *Constellation* in such disrepair, an electrical engineer who lived locally but worked in Manhattan as the lead electrical engineer for Bloomberg, volunteered his weekends to re-wiring the boat for me. I was humbled again as *Constellation's* switch box was re-wired, new gadgets added to make my life easier, the joy of having someone be so generous with their time - it was also a joy to have someone else to work with on *Constellation*, an act which had always been a hard, mostly lonely endeavour. As *Constellation* was rewired, Mike put a diesel engineer onto my engine which was soon fixed after a good clean and service. Walter, the head rigger at Brewers organised a full re-rig of the boat, including a new rolling furler and modifications to my sails from the local Doyle sailmakers, modifying my old-style hanks to manage my foresail configuration from the cockpit. No more straddling myself on the forepeak with a rusty pair of pliers - I could just unroll the jib from the cockpit - what luxury!

Constellation had remained virtually unchanged from her original factory setup - other than the addition of a windvane for self-steering, the boat was stock-standard, just as Jeremy Rogers had built her in 1972. While all this work was going on, the snow piled up, I found online work, and earned enough to survive and save for the trucking portion of *Constellation's* next leg of the journey.

For the second time in my life, I had a girlfriend, finally being able to overcome the relationship which had disintegrated over a year earlier. She lived in Brooklyn and I ended up traveling backwards and forwards along Long Island by bus, as nights on *Constellation* had become unbearable in the snow. The comforts of land, a relationship and living close to the greatest city on earth were enticing and difficult to leave. I flew home to Australia for six weeks, seeing friends and family I hadn't seen for years, taking the opportunity to make money and work whenever possible, organising trucking quotes and additional logistics and finances to move my little boat 3000 miles across the country.

Even after all the miles I had sailed and the situations I had overcome, I still felt a lot of fear about the Pacific. Life was getting more and more comfortable everyday. I wondered why I needed to keep pushing forward - I began to consider what additional gains would there be in crossing the Pacific ocean too? The strong sense that maybe it was luck which had gotten me this far was palpable. It was as if the more comfort I experienced, the greater my sense of fear grew - the connection between comfort and fear becoming inseparable. It was as if comfort was a physical object which made me feel safe, that I didn't want to lose or give up for fear I would have nothing. These feelings were hard to manage, as I understood my own psychology and fear getting in the way of my desire for adventure and to finish what I had set out to achieve. It was as if the devil were on my shoulder, enticing me into a comfortable and nice life in New York, eating nice food, having a girlfriend, friends... My management of fear, the sense of wholeness and connectedness with the ocean and the sky, was waning, the material distractions and comforts clouding my judgement and clarity. With voyaging so far, everything was such a tremendous up and down: on land my ups and downs were about how to continue, they were future-thinking, constantly battling the logistics of money and time. But at sea, I continued to have the same sense of up and down, but the issues at hand were more real, they were about survival, about my interaction and management of my own emotions in a much larger and real sense. So, in a way it was not an escape from reality at sea, or a place where everything was at peace or in a constant state of calm - the truth is, the emotional burden of it all continued but in a more manageable and human sense. Perhaps in a holistic or spiritual way of thinking, time at sea didn't alleviate the problems of life, but the problems that did exist were present, raw and real. In contrast, time spent on land was often about battling more petty emotions, seemingly pointless problems (in the grand scheme of things) and juggling complex relationships. In essence, this life on land with all its trappings lacked a certain depth - everything was trivial. It was almost impossible to find the present moment whilst constantly distracted and wrapped up in the day to day and with no great expansive and meditative horizons to reconnect me to a more aware state of mind.

As spring arrived, I moved more permanently back to Greenport. Walter, who worked for the marina and had been a great supporter of my trip, offered me a free room in his rented house while I continued work on *Constellation*. My electrical engineer friend Mari loaned me his spare Ford pickup and before long I was commuting 10 minutes every day to the yard, stopping for donuts and coffee along with all the other tradesmen, wearing burly work coats and driving similarly blue collar Fords. A trucking company had been organised for the boat, a deadline now firmly written in the sand, and this made all the jobs and work move along much more swiftly and with greater purpose. Jack had booked flights from Berlin to New York, as we planned to drive across the U.S while *Constellation* was trucked in parallel. His arrival brought back the energy and sense that things were underway, the project was continuing and my brief life here in New York was coming to an end.

My relationship in Brooklyn was showing signs of distress. It felt impossible to consider how I could keep going on this adventure while also maintaining a relationship with someone back in New York. Her name was Lisa and we had known each other since university in Australia where she was studying as an exchange student from New York some years previous. Lisa looked at me on the couch and asked me point blank: 'do you only like me because I like you?'. I did enjoy being adored by someone. It was messy. I was confused. It was only my second relationship and there was an undercurrent of sabotage happening on my end of the bargain because I knew I was going to have to break this off in order to continue. Ultimately, I was weak, and said 'no, I really like you'... And cruelly dragged it on.

OVERLAND U.S.A

Now 550 days into the voyage (not counting the year it took to pay for the boat), Jack reminded me with laughter that at the beginning of filming, sitting in a cafe in Berlin, I had estimated it would take me between six and nine months to complete the voyage. We now sat aboard *Constellation* in New York, the snow melting through the scuppers as we planned our route across the U.S. We flew into Denver so we would arrive on the Pacific side at around the same time as *Constellation*. In parallel to my trip across the country, my brother had flown back in from Australia to ride a motorcycle from Texas to Alaska. The motorcycle in question was actually a gift to me from someone following my voyage, who took pity upon my brazen idea of riding a bicycle across the country and offered me a free motorcycle instead. The logistics and additional cost of a motorcycle trip were untenable, so my brother took ownership of the bike and proceeded north to Alaska.

Once in Denver, Jack rented a car and I came down with a horrific flu. We drove across the beautiful American landscape in our white rental car. Channelling a kind of Werner Herzog sensibility, we traversed the Rocky Mountains, camouflaged in the white snow. Our trip was quintessentially American; diners, $50 motels and hamburgers. After 10 days on the road, we made it to Berkeley, California, only to find *Constellation* hadn't even been picked up. Jack soon left, on deadline with work projects back in Berlin. I remained pondering my living situation, not knowing anyone in the greater San Francisco area, nor having a place to live without *Constellation*.

Much earlier in the voyage, I was emailed by someone about my age named Ted, offering any help if I ever made it to the west coast. At the time of the email, I was still in Europe and the idea of New York and the overland trip was not even a seeded thought. Without anything to lose, I reached out to Ted, who now had a small daughter and lived aboard his boat with his family near Berkeley. Astonishingly, he responded quickly, offering me a place to stay on a boat his parents owned nearby but never used. I was over the moon with gratitude, genuinely considering buying a tent at Walmart and camping for the estimated three weeks it was now going to take for *Constellation* to arrive. Ted invited me to a bonfire at the nearby marina, organised by fellow liveaboards from the Bay Area. I felt surrounded by my people - all sorts of curious characters were living on boats here in the counterculture capital of the world.

Constellation did eventually arrive, towed by a Dodge RAM and a dual axle trailer, which to my mind was an undersized combination for such a long haul. Nevertheless, *Constellation* was here, the driver exclaiming he only just made it, his automatic transmission being pushed to virtual destruction while towing across the peaks of Colorado. *Constellation* was a heavy boat by design, yet she was also my home, full of spare parts and additional equipment, being perhaps heavier than everyone expected. Surrounded by curious onlookers as *Constellation* was dropped into the water by crane, I quickly dabbed her underside with antifoul on the hoist, re-attached the rudder and prayed the engine would start. Ted came across and helped, the engine miraculously coming to life as we motored over to a slip near his boat for the big job of putting everything back together.

My days in Berkeley were fun. I met dozens of new people and many generous souls offered to help get things ready for my Pacific crossing. We lashed *Constellation* to the side of Ted's boat, a vessel two thirds larger than my own and a significantly taller mast. Using his mast with a complex array of lines and winches, we managed to step the mast from the dock, a rather precarious job to be undertaking with other boats so close. This was the first time the rig was going up after significant work had been done back in New York, including the addition of the furler, along with all new standing rigging and custom made reinforced chain plates. The boat came together with all of the new work and systems fully functioning. In addition to all the boat work, I'd managed to buy a very small laptop, which after much fiddling I was able to connect to my satellite phone, giving me the ability to download weather data en route, as well as send email & update my blog remotely. My hope was that the weather would be a great boon to my sailing and confidence, finally being able to see what was going on around me. Although, as time would tell, the stress of knowing what was to come without being able to do anything about it was more stressful than this new technology was worth!

The endless jobs to complete before my departure continued, until the list began to run dry, signalling that I would actually have to start sailing again. I went on a day trip with my friend Adam, also a Contessa 26 aficionado and a wonderful help along the way, along the Pacific coast. Standing on a cliff edge, I looked out into the Pacific, full of fear and dread. A wave of anxiety swept over me as I realised the jobs on *Constellation* were done and all the distractions of New York, the logistics and seemingly endless amount of work it took to get there was all coming to a head. After all these years of having Australia in my sights, I was separated by only a single ocean - the largest one of them all.

The wind was cold. Mark Twain famously stated the coldest winter he had ever had was a summer in San Francisco. Transfixed on the Pacific horizon, all the thoughts and emotion from my crossing of the Atlantic rushed back, the feelings as palpable as if I was still there, stuck in the Gulf Stream or mid-Atlantic, laying on the cabin sole in my sleeping bag, tears in my eyes at the endless rolling and existential dread of it all. Why was it so easy to remember the negative emotions of my voyaging? Why could I not recall the bliss, which, if looked at statistically, far outweighed all this negative thinking? It was a conundrum. I suppose there was still much internal work for me to do. Adam left me in peace, knowing full well from his own experiences in sailing solo to Hawaii that I was processing a lot of internal conflict. Like the many men I'd met in marinas along the way, clutching endless job lists as the excuse for not departing tomorrow, I too had been holding onto the security of not sailing, washed up in the distraction of preparation. We walked back to the car and drove home to Sausalito where we were now berthed, a place I really didn't want to leave. I rarely felt at home anywhere in the world, but for whatever reason, Sausalito felt right. Whether it was because I was subconsciously trying to make myself feel truly at home so I could avoid thinking about any more sailing, or whether there was something intrinsic about the place I couldn't say... Sausalito was an iconic and salty home for many revolutionary voyagers, including Sterling Hayden and Bernard Moitessier. I couldn't class myself with those men, but there was an undeniable, seafaring energy to the place which holds my heart to this day.

The support and generosity continued, with a buddhist monk named Dawa coming to visit me in Sausalito in the days before my departure, bringing a shopping bag of provisions for my voyage as a gift. Ladonna and Rob, instrumental friends in the Bay Area, joked they would help me out with 25lbs of beans and rice the first time I met them - a promise they made good on. They also ferried me about, helping onboard with a myriad of projects, as well as writing about me in the popular local sailing magazine, Latitude 38, which brought further interest and support to my voyage. Within days, they also towed me out under the Golden Gate bridge, my engine working but for whatever reason unable to push the boat past about 3.8kts of speed. With a little help from my friends, we broke free of the currents under the bridge and set sail, performing a little test voyage down to Half Moon Bay, a small coastal town south of San Francisco which would be my final point of departure bound for Hawaii.

A small flotilla of friends sailed with me past Mavericks and into the anchorage of Half Moon Bay. Rafted up at anchor, we spent the weekend hunting for crab, watching sailing movies and eating clam chowder. It was a great feeling to finally be ready for departure, no longer toiling away on the boat, just enjoying being with my friends. By Sunday, everyone left, as we studied weather charts and decided I wasn't actually going to be able to leave for another five days. Alone and at anchor, my mind had time to wonder again, no longer distracted by endless preparation. I tried to spend as much time as I could off the boat, walking around Half Moon Bay or sitting in one of the restaurants with a bottomless mug of coffee, but the reality was the pre-departure anxiety was hard to manage. I just didn't have a good feeling, along with the knowledge that the first 4 days out of California were going to most likely be cold and hard. The sense that I was pushing my luck simply wouldn't leave me, as if I had walked across a suspended tightrope and made it, about to return across the rope but for what reason? I had already attained the knowledge and experience from doing it once. How many times does one need to do something to know they can do it? This kind of round-robin anxiety driven thinking was sending me up a wall. I knew full-well I needed to just leave, get out there and return to my happy place instead of grasping on to every little fearful emotion which passed by my synapses. I thought about Lisa, how badly I had treated her, the relationship eventually gasping its final breaths and ending. I was a menace on land, that was the truth.

By now it was June, placing me late into the season yet again, much like my Atlantic crossing. Because of my lateness, the decision was made with the help of my friends that I should aim for Hawaii, rather than my initial route of exploring French Polynesia, which was one of the major highlights of the entire trip. I'd read Kontiki along with Moitessier, Hayden, Robert Louis Stevenson and Jack London throughout the voyage, forever-daydreaming of spending months amongst uninhabited atolls and islands. This wasn't to be the reality of this voyage, though. As we set sail, my friend Adam returned down the coast to buddy-boat with me out into the Pacific.

We sailed in unison, chatting over the radio as I pointed *Constellation's* bow out into the void of coastal low visibility. Adam eventually peeled away and headed back north of the Golden Gate, chatting on VHF until the signal no longer carried our words. Before long, the dreadful reality of my aloneness covered me like a cold blanket. *Constellation* sailed without emotion, providing a kind of bedrock to set myself against. For a full 36 hours I couldn't eat and barely slept, the dread of sailing off a continent into the world's largest ocean was inexplicable.

Laying in my bunk, I simply held still, fighting away the dread, telling myself I just needed time to re-adjust to my environment and situation, relying on the healing properties of time. With joy, time did begin to heal my fears, and I started to re-imagine the Pacific as my new home, embracing its emptiness and rekindling my joy afloat. The Atlantic held another kind of emotional sensibility, as if it was a busier, less remote place - a place bookended by significant landmass on either side - the Pacific felt limitless.

INTO THE PACIFIC

In the book '*A Voyage for Madmen*', Peter Nichols speaks about the driving factors behind the men who raced in the first Golden Globe Race, the first nonstop, singlehanded voyage around the world. Nichols classifies the archetypal solo sailor as being driven by a combination of 'imagination, self-discipline, selfishness, endurance, fear, courage and social instability'. These hallmarks rang true, with a full ocean ahead of the bow to contemplate them all, as we finally broke free of the Pacific high and entered the tradewinds.

The first three days out of California put me sailing above 30 degrees north in conditions similar to my voyage into the North Atlantic, the variable belt of the *Horse latitudes*. With twin jib sails set and a full mainsail up, we began to make good progress, although the cost of progress with this sail configuration was an incessant rolling, a problem I was forever trying to resolve in order to make my life more comfortable. The squalls seemed more unpredictable and more constant than the Atlantic. Innocuous looking cloud formations, which I would normally have been unconcerned about, rattled through with a concerning force.

On the fourth night, asleep in my bunk, my radar detector sounded. This small device often carried by French solo sailors detects the radar of other ships, as often boats of this size cannot actually be seen by radar, or they are indistinguishable from waves or general weather phenomena. The reality is that commercial deep-sea shipping cannot reliably have a human monitoring the radar screen 24x7 for six weeks at a time. Therefore, assuming these big ships have their radar switched on at all times, this little device aboard *Constellation* will ring out with a terrible tone when it senses one, forcing you awake.

When crossing oceans, the device rarely ever sounds. These oceans are so remote, the chances of crossing paths with anything other than a fish or some flotsam are slim. Because of this, when it does sound, there is an immediate adrenaline rush as one jumps into the cockpit to see where the vessel is. Set with a fairly high sensitivity, the ship in question was still a long way off. By my visual calculations and reading of the vessel's lights, the ship also appeared to be well off of a collision course, sailing much faster and on a parallel course to mine. I reduced the sensitivity of the radar detector and went back to sleep - shortly afterwards, the device sounded again, even at its minimum setting. With confidence the ship wasn't a risk, I switched the unit off and returned to sleep, an erroneous decision with huge consequences.

Constellation shook from bow to stern and rail to rail. The deep rumble of engines and bright lights pulled me from a dream state into a hell state, as the sight of a huge tanker bared down onto me. Everything lit up as powerful deck lights on the tanker illuminated the cockpit. I dove on to the tiller, crash jibing to port, away from the oncoming bow. The tanker, towering multiple stories above me, rushed past. The huge bow wake caused *Constellation* to rock with such force that I nearly fell out of the cockpit. While I'd avoided being directly hit, we rounded up behind this enormous ocean-going behemoth as its wake sucked us in - I rushed to the mainsheet to tighten the mainsail and steady us. In enormous shock and feeling an incredible sense of luck, we continued to roll in the wake as I stood watching the tanker fly off into the horizon. I replayed the whole scenario over and over again in my head at light speed whilst blindly fumbling with the rudder, adrenaline coursing through me, my hands shaking.

I quickly snapped back to the present, grabbing the VHF radio and screaming an almost primal scream down the radio. To which I heard no reply. I continued to try and make contact with the vessel and gave up in disgust, knowing full well these ships were running without watch. On the one hand it was hypocritical of a solo sailor to be mad with another vessel for not maintaining a proper watch. However, in a sense I felt a collision due to poor watch keeping on my end could probably not cause the same harm this tanker could. *Constellation* was so small and so slow, I genuinely wondered whether anyone would even notice if I ran directly into a tanker.

Out of nowhere, a voice on the radio stated the name of the tanker, to which I replied that they had almost hit me. The watch keeper took a moment and said he could not see any trace of me anywhere on radar, which was unsurprising, and I reminded him that he was meant to be keeping a visual watch. He shrugged my comment off and asked where I was headed. His contribution to the conversation after nearly killing me was that Oahu was full of nice girls. I laughed in a polite but shocked way and asked where he was headed - the tanker was bound for South America from Hong Kong - six weeks at sea. The reality is, these vessels run ocean passages under minimal visual watch and I imagined the crew down below playing XBox.

As if I wasn't already bathing in a sea of existential dread about the Pacific and the purpose of it all, this new event solidified the pointlessness and luck of the endeavour. The tanker only had to be off course by a fraction of a degree to have completely run me over, and I couldn't forgive myself for the mistake I'd made. The reality was, it was all my fault, every moment of it: I had chosen to do this, I had chosen to ignore the radar alert, I had chosen to go back to sleep, I knew the risks. This core reality, the truth that I had no one else to blame for anything, was one of the greatest lessons I had grappled with the entire voyage - those days in the Atlantic where

I punched the mast in moments of frustration and loneliness, on the verge of insanity, perhaps on the brink of something greater, it was often hard to tell which was which. In a more sedentary life, it's possible to exist and place blame everywhere but with oneself - but out here, who can you blame for anything? One lives the life of a small god as a solo sailor, living in a reality of one's own control and one's own full responsibility. Yes, a tanker could run you down (and you may not have been in control of that vessel), however you were in control of the fact you were there in the first place, exposing yourself to such risk. The truth is, if you place yourself in harm's way, survival is a combination of luck, fortitude and planning - two you have some semblance of control over, the third you have virtually none - 33% of your survival is entirely up to the cosmos.

For two days I sailed with a heavy mind, unable to forgive myself for my mistake, deciding I would end the voyage in Hawaii. The risk was too great and I was not sailing with the kind of seamanship required to be out doing this thing. The trades blew me along and now that I was able to see the weather data I could download. My track under the Pacific High, I was in a belt of steady 12-15kt winds. My mind lightened as time went on, but the resolve to quit in Hawaii remained.

After my scare with the tanker, I began running the mast light with a full strobe effect every night. This strobing part of the tri-light at the top of the mast was an addition made while the rigging was being redone, however it was technically reserved for emergencies.

The incident had spooked me to the point where I simply wanted to be seen, at all cost. Nearing the islands of Hawaii, I sat becalmed one night, as *Constellation* ground to a complete standstill without wind. With the strobe on, I lay asleep in my bunk, before hearing the unusual crackling of the radio as a nearby vessel called for the '*yacht in distress*'. I knew immediately this call was for me, jumping on deck to the sight of yet another tanker right by my side, yet this time, also at a complete standstill. Here we were, two vessels stopped in the middle of the ocean, my strobe flashing like a nightclub in the dead of night. The captain was friendly and concerned, as I explained the purpose of the strobe was to ensure I wasn't nearly hit again because of an earlier incident. The captain understood, continuing to ask if everything was ok. Assuring everything was, the tanker slowly fired back up and moved on its way. The kindness and sea-manly concern of the ship's captain buoyed my spirits as landfall neared.

The sun began to set in picturesque tropical tradewind orange fashion, as *Constellation* flew into Honolulu under full sail in a brisk localised sea breeze. A sunset cruising catamaran full of tourists whipped by, Michael Jackson playing at full bore. After a full 27 days at sea, the passage had taken 7 days more than I had anticipated, due to my inability to find my way out of the Pacific High and into proper trades. We had made it - I could finally quit this voyage and move on. Maybe Lisa would take me back. I could move to New York?

A surf break white-capped on one side of the entrance buoy into Waikiki, with a break wall on the other. The engine spluttered and we maintained full sail in case we lost power - so at least I might have a chance to pull out of the entrance and sail back out to sea. With luck we made it in, surrounded by locked gates in the quarantine/check-in area. Thankfully another cruising boat was also in the same predicament, motioning I tie up alongside and wait till morning for customs clearance. With significant gratitude, my new friends Sherri and Gene handed me a cold beer, a plate of rice and sautéed mushrooms atop a piece of Australian lamb. The reality of reaching home started to dawn on me for the first time, the chart on my chart table showing a significant chunk of the Pacific knocked off in this single passage.

The process of checking in was like anywhere else, as I navigated the vintage halls, cubicles and offices of the customs and quarantine building, located at nearby Pearl Harbour. In a lot of ways, Honolulu was, for a better word, outdated, giving off a sense that not much had changed aesthetically since the 1980s. Office workers wore brightly coloured Hawaiian shirts with complete seriousness, huddling around their buildings to smoke at lunchtime.

Through an unexpected connection, I got in contact with a woman named Nicole, the program director for Roz Savage, a British woman attempting to row around the world who had recently left the islands. Through Nicole, I was introduced to the Waikiki Yacht Club

(WYC), who graciously offered to host my visit in Honolulu. The offer was uncanny, as I raced around the public dock trying to find a vacant slip to no avail. Hawaii is a difficult place to have a boat, with few natural anchorages which offer protection from the constant howl of the trades. With access to all of the WYC facilities, I spent the majority of my days working on my computer from a table overlooking the ocean. My finances had been more or less exhausted by the trans-America trip, however the online work I'd manage to secure in New York continued, with a flexible time arrangement allowing me to work when I was available. It was the ideal scenario, even though it was only just enough money to survive. The foresail which was converted from hanks to the new furler system had been destroyed on the passage from California, requiring a complete replacement. As luck would have it, a regular follower of my voyage was also a sailmaker, offering to build me a new working jib at cost. I immediately jumped at the deal, nervously taking all of the required measurements on the mast with a small ruler and a piece of rope.

The initial days of my stay in Honolulu were not unusual, although I still regularly contemplated the idea of completely throwing the towel in on the whole trip. However, as these things go, the feeling of accomplishment in making it safely, along with the generosity being shown already in port, I started to think less and less of abandonment and more about my departure plans, given the oncoming hurricane season...

One evening I was asked whether I wanted to go twilight racing on someone else's boat. I generally say no to such offers, simply because I've never thought of myself as a particularly good sailor or a good team member on a boat. Racing is always so stressful. However, the offer was coming from the commodore of the yacht club, so it wasn't one I could necessarily decline! That evening, we sailed off out of Waikiki with a handful of people I'd never met. I regaled tales of my time at sea to an interested audience in the cockpit, avoiding any hints to help in the actual sailing of the boat - I could not have been less interested in trimming or hoisting the spinnaker for the downward run.

The relationship with Lisa was over. The story of it all perhaps requires an entire chapter, the ending for which I was entirely to blame. The real difficulty with meeting people along the way (in particular women) was the nature of my adventure - ultimately it was a personal voyage of self-discovery, a kind of quest, and the singlehanded nature of it all had been part of it from the very beginning. So the reality was, if I did meet someone who could put up with me (and vice versa), what was I to do? In a sense I was exhausted by all this alone-time. New York had spoiled me - it had made my constitution weak. In honesty, the relationship with Lisa had ended because of a multitude of selfish interests and pursuits. I was in love with both the idea of myself as a courageous solo voyager but also the newfound interest from people following my journey - some of whom were attractive young women. I barely acted on any of it, but I wanted to pursue what it might avail to me, if I were honest. In the end, it probably meant further coming to terms with the fact that a part of me is desperate for love - that I love to be loved - but truthfully the deep vulnerability and accountability to another person is a hell of a lot harder. In short, I was young.

I should never have gone into or indicated I was open to a relationship with someone on this voyage - but alas, I had - I was human and who doesn't want love. While twilight sailing, I began talking with a girl named Jess, who was sharp, funny and tomboyish. I had a sinking feeling later that night as I lay awake in *Constellation*, thinking about the day that I'd shown too much interest, asked too many questions and probably opened myself up to further personal relationship dramas.

Sure enough, the next day, Jess had tracked me down on Facebook and invited me to a friend's birthday party. I accepted her invitation, which led to days and then weeks of hanging out together. She was a lawyer with an apartment in Waikiki, overlooking the beach, where I ended up staying as opposed to remaining onboard *Constellation*, before taking the bus to my boat to work during the day. Jess worked in a privileged position with a local judge of some renown. The days and weeks went by more quickly than they should have, as my addiction to comfort and companionship etched away at my goals and ambitions. It was New York all over again. Why was I doing this to myself? Why was I doing this to others?

At long last, the new working jib arrived, fitting

perfectly to my great relief. With the new sail and repairs to the engine, I decided to take a sailing trip up the west coast of Oahu, to Waimea Bay, which at this time of year was completely flat and perfect for anchoring (becoming one of the world's largest waves during the winter season). With Jess onboard, we sailed around the west coast, stopping at anchorages along the way, eating fresh poké from corner stores and food trucks, diving off the bow and endlessly talking. The lee of the island caused a virtual calm from a sailing perspective, the light conditions providing glassy seas and slow progress to Waimea - yet without a real timeline, there wasn't a bother in the world.

Sailing with Jess was fun. She proved to be inquisitive, easy going, and adaptable to living onboard such a small, cramped and uncomfortable space. Reaching Waimea, we anchored for two days, swimming amongst the turtles and paddling ashore to buy provisions, ferrying them back to the boat on a surfboard Adam had gifted me back in Sausalito. Returning along the coast, we rounded Barbers Point, which was our entrance directly into the northeast trade winds for the return leg to Waikiki. The conditions were absolutely miserable, the engine running at full tilt as we pounded into a heavy tradewind sea. The weather, wind and water was warm, but the misery remained, Jess huddling in the cockpit while managing to remain positive, as I navigated through the transition from calm waters to pounding waves. Her positivity and helpfulness over the week of sailing made an impression on me. We eventually motored into the yacht club, utterly drenched, the bunks sopping wet, sleeping bags weighed down with water, the bilge pump gushing warm ocean water back out of the drains. My loss of grit and addiction to comfort reared its head. I tied *Constellation* up without properly cleaning out the week's mess and we immediately left for Jess's apartment - *Constellation* neglected.

The U.S had been kind to me, as I thought more and more about the reality of reaching home, wondering what on earth I was going to do when I finally did reach this mythical destination I'd been working so hard to reach. Hawaii felt like a significant milestone and '*home*' was beginning to make me feel anxious. After years of effort and work, it was quite a real possibility this whole life might be over. Part of me relished the idea of it all ending, being able to move onto something new, while another part of me began to realise the constant pushing and never ending challenges were really what made my life worth living. Without the voyage, without the challenge, I wondered what was left? Without any interest in pursuing a traditional career, broke, unmarried and unhindered with just a small boat and a few stories, what was a man to do?

Overlooking Waikiki beach watching the sunset one evening, Jess turned to me and asked me to marry her. I was surprised, but also I enjoyed the insanity of the idea: we'd only known each other for about a month, but I loved doing whatever was the craziest thing to do. So, in the spirit of craziness, I simply replied, '*sure, why not?*'. The answer '*why not*' was really a key moment in this all, because in my existential dread of nearly being hit with a tanker in the weeks prior, coupled with my overthinking about what I was going to do next, or what the point of it all was, now seemed to have been answered: I'd simply get married and become part of Jess's life.

We'd spoken idly about the idea of me living in the U.S, even reaching out to immigration lawyers previously to see if there was any way to reinstate a childhood green card I'd had (which wasn't possible). So, this marriage idea also had the practical outcome of being able to live in the U.S., while solving my '*what next*' question. Being engaged also seemed to be a partial answer to my ever-present existentialism. What better way to solve a pit of loneliness - instead of solving the *where* and *why* of that particular problem - *just get married!* It seemed to work for everyone else - or so I told myself sarcastically. I did think at the time that I loved Jess, that wasn't a lie - however I suppose it would take me some more time to realise that the power of chemical attraction in the first months often makes you feel like the relationship is perfect and destined for greatness. Relationships, of course, can take many months to develop and reveal themselves to us and building a solid foundation takes time. In hindsight, I was barely ready for a relationship, much less marriage.

So here I was, living halfway between the Waikiki Yacht Club, an apartment with a girl I'd just got engaged to, overlooking Waikiki beach, still several thousands of nautical miles from the destination I'd set my sights on and committed to reaching several years before. While Jess was at work, I'd tinker away on *Constellation* and go to the local mall and drink iced coffee to defog my brain from the incessant heat. This was the same mall we'd gone to just a week earlier to buy matching silver engagement rings from a cheap jeweller - $80/each. In an odd way, the engagement had solidified the fact I was still going to push on for Australia, as planned. It provided a renewed sense that there was something at the end of it all, giving me a morale boost. Jess also encouraged me, even though it would mean many months apart and many unknowns. Her time in Hawaii would be coming to a close anyway, as she returned to U.C Davis to finish some studies before heading to Washington D.C to work in humanitarian law. I began working on *Constellation* in earnest, keeping a sharp eye on the weather and preparing my route across the remainder of the Pacific ocean.

On that twilight yacht race where I had met Jess, I also met another woman, a marine biologist who worked on the famed Palmyra Atoll research station, some 900 miles south of Oahu, quite literally in the middle of nowhere. I'd seen this tiny atoll on charts previously, friends in California also mentioning I should try and figure out a way to visit (it was now a private island, requiring special permission). I reached out to the biologist and began working on the paperwork and permissions to visit, which at the time were not too arduous (having since changed significantly). With permission to visit and the looming expiration of my U.S visa just days away, the pressure was on to leave.

With added time pressure, a major category 4 hurricane was headed to the islands of Hawaii. It was August now, coming into peak hurricane season, with few (if any) yachts leaving for more southerly latitudes. Yet again, I was late and at risk of destabilised weather, a common theme I never seemed to be able to shake. Days later as I watched charts and the media talk up the hurricane, I walked into the customs office with my passport, exclaiming my visa was about to expire and I couldn't leave due to hurricane activity in the Pacific. The attending officer was friendly and didn't think twice about stamping my passport for another six months. Upon exit, thoughts of delaying my departure reared again... But I knew, deep inside, if I delayed another moment, I'd be wrapped up in a whole other life, trapping myself and avoiding everything I had worked so hard to achieve thus far.

As the hurricane dissipated on approach to Hawaii, it became time to start organising my departure in earnest. The situation with Jess became more stressed as my departure became imminent. *Constellation* was completely re-provisioned from Costco, mostly full of rubbish food I regretted buying in hindsight: can upon can of beef stew, dozens of packets of beef jerky and an endless supply of cinnamon porridge. On a calm day against the trades, I said my goodbyes to friends and supporters, sailing across to Kaneohe Bay. Whenever possible, I would say goodbye to all my friends and sail somewhere quiet for a night or two before my official departure. Sailing through the aptly named '*Crashboat Channel*' into the Bay, I found a nice anchorage for the night, before proceeding over to the Kaneohe yacht club to see Jess before I left.

Jess sat down on the bunk down below, looked at me, and said she was coming with me. One of the ongoing emotions I'd struggled with was not the aloneness of sailing itself, but the aloneness of arriving in a place and not having someone to share it with. I'd often dreamt of what it might be like to sail into a tiny atoll in the middle of nowhere, with a partner, or even just a friend, pondering how different my experience would be. More and more it seemed there were two parts to sailing for me: on the one hand, I loved the solitude of ocean crossings, but despised my landfall, having no one to share the joy of discovery with. I selfishly enjoyed my solitude at sea, but selfishly wanted someone to share the other end of the journey with, as long as that person didn't disrupt the sailing portion! My whims, emotions and desires seemed impossible to satisfy. With all this going through my head, I once again said '*why not*', and immediately my life dramatically changed.

It was a Friday and Jess said she could be ready to sail by Monday, knowing full-well the urgency and calm before another hurricane started barreling up from Mexico. One of the things I loved about Jess was her gumption and ability to get things done: she had just committed to packing up her entire life and apartment into storage within two days - and then committed to sailing off over the horizon with someone she had only known for six weeks and to whom she was now engaged! It was all madness, but exciting at the same time. This all completely changed the dynamic of my trip - it also completely ended the solo aspect of it, and I'd now jeopardised my initial commitment, feeling deeply guilty. *I'd lasted this long! I'd pushed so hard!* But in hindsight, the reality was, I couldn't fight against my loneliness for another moment. I was vulnerable after the near collision, lonely, and frankly, Jess was a real go-getter - it also felt like I might actually start enjoying myself for a change - the introspection was becoming exhausting - I often wondered how deep down the hole of neurosis I'd ventured into went.

Jess had friends in Apia, Western Samoa as well as commitments back at U.C Davis, so the idea was that she would sail with me on this leg to Samoa, and fly out back to California. The weekend was intense, Jess going in to work on a Saturday to tell the judge she'd worked for that was leaving to sail across the Pacific with a man she'd just met. Surprisingly the judge, while disappointed, showed a twinkle in his eye - to be young.

By the end of Saturday, she'd procured a pickup truck from a friend and organised a storage unit as we packed up her belongings. *Constellation* was already over-provisioned, so the addition of someone else for the next few weeks posed no supply issues. That Monday, we motored out of Crashboat Channel and back into the depths of the Pacific Ocean.

PALMYRA & BEYOND

It was now mid-August and we were underway, bound for Palmyra atoll. My voyage was well-followed on the Internet, with regular updates via my blog, tracking page and Twitter. The addition of Jess to the trip was mindfully removed from my posts. It felt disingenuous to my audience, but on the other hand, this was also my private life and many private things happened along the way which I didn't speak about publicly: this ended up being one of them. Jess, the stowaway.

The first three days out of Kaneohe Bay were slow in calm conditions. A large swell ran, built by hurricane winds outside of our direct region. The peaks and troughs of the swell were enormous, perhaps the largest I'd ever experienced - *Constellation* sank deep down into the troughs as I looked up from the cockpit to the stern, watching the enormity of the wave pass under us. Jess was oblivious to the kinds of conditions to expect. She had no offshore sailing experience and didn't know the waves were out of the ordinary. Not mentioning anything so as not to strike fear into her soul, I felt the new emotion of responsibility onboard: previously, I had no one to be responsible for, if I made mistakes, fell overboard, or became caught up in a situation that I was unable to handle, these were all my own problems, and I had no one else to blame. Ultimate personal responsibility - yet, with Jess onboard, I felt a deep responsibility to keep her safe, which started to grind me down. Sailing alone was stressful enough, yet now I had allowed additional stress onboard inadvertently. In my poor forward thinking and proper consideration of the idea, I began to beat myself up for jeopardising the nature of my trip and taking on extra responsibility. Perhaps, I began to consider, my selfishness knew no bounds.

The weather fluctuated between high winds, big seas, brief moments of trade wind sailing and back again. With access to weather data onboard, I nervously tracked another tropical storm hovering to the east, most likely responsible for the swell and unreliable weather. The ocean seemed bare, with no flying fish or friendly Mahi glistening in the sun. Had the Pacific been fished out? Watching the historical footage of Thor Heyderahl aboard Kontiki, enormous whale sharks swimming underneath their raft, countless Tuna and big game fish being caught with regularity, it was hard not to think the Pacific had been pillaged.

Now within the Inter Tropical Convergence Zone (ITZC, commonly referred to as the equatorial doldrums), unpredictable conditions were the rule not the exception. The searing heat was almost unbearable as we spent time outside in the cockpit at sunrise, retreating down below soon after as the sun belted down. During the late evenings, we'd return on deck, the heat captive in *Constellation's* core, re-radiating throughout the night till it all started again the next morning. Someone had given us a DVD player and every season of The West Wing, a political drama set in the White House. As the days rolled by, we lay down below, our sheets soaked in sweat, distracted by the machinations of dramatised American politics. In between we would read, simply stare at the cabin roof, talk, or as would happen more frequently, argue.

To most sane people, the idea of confining oneself to a 26ft boat alone with a person you'd only recently met (and become engaged to) for upwards of a month with no escape seems like a really terrible idea. But to a lonely sailor riding highs and lows, displaying clear emotional instability, it seemed like a great idea. That is, until we were well beyond the point of return, surrounded by hurricanes en route to an atoll 3ft above sea level, in the middle of nowhere.

The joy of long passages is that they reconnect you with your environment and allow you to think beyond yourself into nature. The present is demanded of you, because time itself slows down, presenting the world as it is without the interference of others. The beginning of this transition is confronting, yet after a week one becomes accustomed to it and any other life almost seems a bit mad. The issue with having Jess onboard, is a week went by and then two, yet the connectedness with the environment and ensuing peace (there were always moments of terror, anger and frustration, however the overwhelming feeling was peaceful and introspective) never arrived. While it was fun to binge watch good TV, the reality was I was normally binge reading deep novels, with sailing actually being a great opportunity to read all those books one finds an excuse not to read on land. The added stress of responsibility, the conflicts onboard as we began to dig back into each other's past to see who we really were, along the lack of connectedness with the natural environment, became more taxing and problematic as the miles towards Palmyra ticked by.

The elephant in the room with Jess was that she was gay. Now, you might be wondering how that was going to work out - so was I. Jess had come out of a 7 year relationship with an older woman not too long before meeting me, and here we were in the middle of the Pacific, engaged and quarrelling about it all. In some sense, there was something exciting about the whole thing, I suppose. Love is a very curious thing, as I pondered the gender-fluidity of it all. It would be a lie not to say this wasn't a bit of an issue for me, deep down. The insecurities I held around her previous relationships with women, how this would play out in our future, as well as big questions around what she saw in me *as a man*, were very confusing. Each relationship I have had before Jess and since has been extremely different and exploratory. I love the depth of experience and there is an addiction to wanting to experience *everything* - my attraction has always been for the multi-faceted - yet with complexity, depth and intense character can also come intense feelings, emotions and a ton of drama and baggage. What is it like to date someone who is gay? Separated? Has kids? Has a personality disorder? Speaks another language? Is stunningly beautiful? Has the intellect of a genius? Came out of a master/slave relationship? Cuts themselves? Believes the Bible as fact? I could tell you, if you were interested.

The mythology and stories of Palmyra atoll were what had drawn me to it. I loved the idea of being able to visit very special places one could never visit otherwise, Palmyra being at the top of my list in the Pacific. It was one of those places people spoke of like an island out of a pirate novel, shrouded in mystery with tales of gold bullion, piracy, war and murder. Only 12 square kilometres in size and less than a metre above sea level, the atoll housed a rotation of scientists, flown in from Honolulu, their planes landing on a runway built from crushed coral during WWII. Discovered by American explorer and sea captain Edmund Fanning, who, while sailing one night had a premonition, instructing his first mate to heave-to and wait till daybreak. That morning, the ship came across the reef of Palmyra within just a mile of the premonition. Had Fanning not stopped the ship on his gut feeling, they most likely all would have perished in a wreck upon the sharp outer reef protecting the atoll. Some four years later, the vessel *USS Palmyra* did shipwreck on the reef, becoming the origin of the name. To date, no signs of settlement from any human populations previous to its discovery have been discovered. Captain Cornelius Sowle of *USS Palmyra* found no inhabitants or freshwater, only an abundance of large coconuts and an exceptional array of fish.

Perhaps the most intriguing story of the island was that of the *Sea Wind* murders. Two couples aboard separate yachts, found themselves alone on Palmyra one season, resulting in a double murder and the theft of *Sea Wind*, the vessel of well-to-do couple Malcolm and Eleanor Graham. The story itself is captivating, the remains of Eleanor discovered in the early 1980s, inside a partially buried and corroded chest found in the lagoon - the discovery by a South African couple visiting by yacht, some four years after the incident. Reading a book written by one of the attorneys inside the sweltering heat of *Constellation's* cabin en route to the atoll was a riveting distraction from the crumbling relationship with Jess.

The trying nature of the voyage to Palmyra was fitting, considering its long and intriguing history, which I pondered over coffee each morning as the equatorial current shipped us east at 2kts, away from the atoll. Eventually after much struggle in squeezing every mile out of the erratic winds, we made it within 31 nautical miles of the island and I attempted to start the engine. To my shock and dismay, the engine refused to start, making new and unusual sounds. Without the need to run the engine on passage because of ample solar energy, it was the first time I'd tried starting it in weeks

- and it was full of white goo. In a panic and with access to very slow and unreliable email, I emailed the mechanic back in New York who had helped me out with the engine. It looked as though an intentional S-bend in the exhaust had flattened out after all the work and transport, which meant water was entering into the engine via the exhaust while underway. The devastation of the discovery was not that the engine may be irreparably damaged, but that the entrance into Palmyra would be virtually impossible without an engine: the perilous coral lined channel which had been blasted by dynamite during the war, was extremely narrow, set against the prevailing winds and filled with sharks.

I spent a dizzying number of hours with my head in the bilge, draining the cream oil into water containers and stashing in the forward compartment. Pouring half a litre of fresh oil back in the engine and cracking the injector to drain the lines with fresh fuel, Jess and I willed the little engine miraculously back to life. I let the oil warm, drained it all again into water containers, topped it back up and motored the final 30 nautical miles towards the channel entrance.

With wide-eyes, Palmyra slowly approached from the East, distant waves crashing on reefs across the horizon, as dozens of new birds, palm lined beaches and evidence of strange looking military structures took shape in the clearing haze. We radioed ahead, noticing an abundance of chatter on the radio as Palmyra marine operations worked on various projects in and around the atoll. Amanda, the Fish and Wildlife representative and refuge manager, answered our call with excitement, as we skirted around the top of the reef, making our way to the infamous channel entrance, renowned for being difficult to find and navigate. Jess stood on the bow, keeping an eye out for coral, searching out any obvious signs of the channel, as we rounded up and took course according to our charts and GPS. Slowly motoring in, an unexpected array of channel markers appeared, being slightly confused by the fact they had been installed backwards, with port and starboard signs reversed. Thankfully Brad, the marine operations manager came out in a tender, guided us safely through the channel.

We had no idea what to expect of the island, how many people were on it or what kind of infrastructure was in place. As we motored closer into the lagoon, a small jetty appeared with several boats tied up, an encampment of bungalows, mess hall, generators, science labs, satellite dishes, sheds, tractors, an air strip and even the world famous Palmyra Yacht Club. Sharks, fish and turtles darted around underneath us, quite literally knocking into the rudder. As Palmyra was a nature reserve, fishing within any significant distance of the atoll was prohibited, preserving nature with abundance.

Constellation was tied to a mooring within West lagoon, right near where the *Sea Wind* murders took place. While sitting in the cockpit, it was possible to see structures outlined in the book which were used for marijuana cultivation by the accused guilty parties of the murder. But I was personally more interested in where the treasure of the *Esperenza* may lay. Gold, silver and pre-Columbian art works were rumoured to have been buried here by shipwrecked crew, so far undiscovered.

Anthony, perhaps the world's most remote chef, invited us to freshly cooked tuna for dinner. Jess and I jumped at the invitation, subsisting primarily on cans of beef stew from Costco which were littered throughout *Constellation*. One of the conditions of visiting Palmyra was we could only come ashore by invitation, and be contactable by radio at all times. Because of its remoteness and function, it was a risk having visitors roaming about unaccounted for. My dream of surfing the outer reef was quashed, as Amanda explained it was simply too risky, an accident requiring a complex, expensive and large-scale rescue out of Honolulu if I impaled myself on a coral head.

We sat around a table at the mess hall, chatting with all the visiting scientists and people who kept the island running. It began to be clear that the island was like a tiny self-contained universe, running in parallel with the rest of the world, thousands of miles away. There were politics, egos and everything else that comes along with humans interacting with each other. It seemed us newcomers provided a helpful distraction from some strained relationships on the island, the current crew coming to an end of their three month rotations - conversely, Jess and I also got an emotional break from each other after weeks in a tiny inescapable space.

Alcohol stores were at an all time low on the island and cigarettes quite literally unobtainable - the only chance of any replenishment was via the barge which visited every six months, through the backpacks of a fresh run of scientists, or the unlikely appearance of a visiting yacht. The only smoker on the island had decided to go cold-turkey by not bringing any tobacco during his roster, finally being driven to the point where he was smoking coconut leaves he would dry on a special oven, cobbled together from WWII artefacts. After dinner we grabbed a bottle of something alcoholic from *Constellation* and the night resumed with music and dancing under a waxing moon in one of the most remote places on earth.

We spent four days on Palmyra, exploring the beaches, the lagoon and the runway. Along the runway were WWII planes and trucks, overgrown in the jungle, looking like props in a movie. The runway itself was lined with enormous liquified gas canons which would fire in succession whenever a plane was en route, scaring the abundant birdlife away long enough for the plane to land. A sign near the runway read '*Palmyra International Airport, population 16*'- the population figure being a changeable number.

Each morning we would radio and ask for permission to come onto the island and explore. While the Nature Conservancy folk were kind enough, one could tell they didn't much like having their universe interrupted. We were outliers on the island and our roaming around seemed to make everyone a little uneasy in a way, which

I suppose was fair enough given we were all strangers to each other. Before the U.S government bought the island (which had apparently also piqued the interest of Bill Gates), a caretaker and his dog used to be the only full time inhabitants, with yachts visiting infrequently outside of the hurricane season. The caretaker was long gone, however his dog, named *Dadu*, was amazingly still around, after a clause was included in the island's sale contract that the dog must remain. *Dadu* had been left for a couple of years between the changeover, surviving entirely on his own by hunting sharks in the shallows. As unbelievable as it sounds, while Jess and I were exploring the shallow waters of a small white sandy beach, *Dadu* wandered down the path, walked into the water and began rounding up small reef sharks like a cattle dog. He didn't attack the sharks any longer, as he was now well fed by the scientists, but it was quite clear he was more than capable if required.

Like many remote islands, sailing visitors like to leave their mark in one way or another. In the Azores, it's a harbour wall, covered in paintings and names of yachts who have passed. In Palmyra, it's a ramshackle building called the Palmyra Yacht Club, full of flags, sailing paraphernalia and discarded fishing balls. Rummaging through *Constellation*, I found a British number plate I'd been carrying all this way for no apparent reason, a broken light buoy, a waterlogged mobile phone and a damp packet of tobacco left onboard by a friend nearly a year prior. I nailed the number plate to the yacht club wall, tacked the tobacco pouch next to it with a note saying '*to be used in extreme emergencies only*', placed the mobile phone on the other side of the club with a note *'call for pizza'* and for reasons I now regret, wrote a soppy love note on the light buoy about Jess, and tied it to the ceiling. I imagine it's all still there to this day, although I do very much hope the light buoy isn't... By the next day, the tobacco was gone - it was no secret who had declared the emergency!

Jess and I more or less took a break from arguing, deciding to enjoy the island, being allowed to only stay for a maximum of seven days. Amazingly, it was possible to get a solid WIFI connection to the Internet from *Constellation* as we floated in the lagoon, allowing me to keep a close eye on the weather. By the fourth day I noticed a perfect belt of sailing weather headed our way, deciding our time on Palmyra must come to a close, so we could begin our voyage to Western Samoa. Saying goodbye to *Dadu* and our island friends, we set sail out of the lagoon and out of the channel on a broad reach, sharks and turtles returning to bid us farewell.

The voyage to Western Samoa was pleasant, at last experiencing stable trade wind conditions. As always, I sailed *Constellation* conservatively, reefing the mainsail, rolling in the jib and soldiering on with less speed through the dark nights, favouring comfort rather than speed. A racing yachtsmen will push their boat around the clock, yet for me, I was simply out here to visit some remote places and read my books - there was no need to stress myself or the boat, which always explained my slow passages. We crossed the equator, popping a bottle of champagne I was given all the way back in New York

City for this very occasion. Without any kind of refrigeration onboard, the champagne was warm and sweet, as we tipped the rest overboard in honour of Poseidon, god of the ocean. I wrote a small story about *Constellation* onto a piece of paper, wrapped it in tin foil, placed it inside the bottle, put the cork back in and threw it overboard. Of my many messages in bottles, unfortunately not one has yet to be returned.

The voyage was lonely in terms of spotting other vessels, with only a tuna clipper and a plane spotted since Hawaii. After a total of 32 days out of Kaneohe Bay, we began our entrance into the port of Apia, Western Samoa. The entrance was perfectly timed for daylight, until an enormous line squall blew across the horizon and destroyed our belt of trades, leaving behind a dead calm, within arms length of Samoa. With only a small amount of diesel left after motoring into Palmyra, we simply had to wait till the wind reappeared. As the hours ticked by and the sun started to set, the water began to show signs of a returning breeze, bringing with it the smell of earth. Out at sea, there is virtually no smell. Or, perhaps there is, but you become so used to it you don't notice it any longer, perhaps because of such little variation. Yet, when approaching landfall, there is almost always a unique aroma which comes along with it. Western Samoa smelt sweet, like flowers and wet earth.

It's always dangerous to enter a port in the dark, however I kept making a habit of it because I was impatient. At 2.30am, I nervously navigated by pure

GPS, listening intently under a dark sky to the sound of crashing waves to starboard. As Palmyra was north of the equator, this was technically my first visit to a South Pacific island. The port authority directed us to anchor, after we moved into the marina the following morning with our yellow quarantine flag flying. As it was a Sunday, all the official offices were closed, but the security kindly let us out of the marina to explore the town regardless which we were grateful for - we couldn't bear the thought of sitting on the boat for the next 24 hours watching people eat ice-cream on the harbour quay as we snacked on two minute noodles straight out of the packet!

After our day exploring Apia, spending the majority of it eating foods of all kinds, Monday rolled around and we were visited by a total of five state departments, including: immigration, health, customs, agriculture and the port authority. It always amused me that the smallest islands had the most complex and far reaching entrance requirements. I thought back to New York where no one had even noticed or seemed to care about my sudden appearance on the shore...

WESTERN SAMOA

Once a week, Jess's father performed in a band which played island music, somewhere in Denver. Because Samoan's were, generally speaking, large, strong people, they would come to the U.S and work as luggage handlers in major airports, with Denver airport being a magnet for Samoan workers for reasons I don't really know (considering the climate!). Like a lot of migrant labourers, they would either send money home to family, or live frugally and save everything they earned, taking it all home when the kitty was large enough. Jess's father had become friends with a Samoan man named Elei, who had returned to Apia to work as a taxi driver after the death of his 20 year old son. We connected with Elei the following day, waiting out front of the Aggie Gray Hotel, a famous gathering place for U.S servicemen in WWII. Elei was a powerful looking man in his 50s, covered in traditional Samoan tattoos. He had *gravitas*, a sense of strength and authority about him, like he should have been leading people into a battle or a boardroom, but he had now been relegated to ferrying tourists around in a yellow car. He insisted on us staying with him at his house instead of the boat, even though I much preferred staying on the boat in almost all circumstances (except for a winter in New York...). There was a deep sense of pride held by Elei - we were on his soil, in his culture and in his house as guests. I was looking forward to having the opportunity to experience the real side of Western Samoa with a local.

Elei pushed Jess and I into a sitting circle of primarily Samoan men at the market, all passing the kava bowl around. Kava, the legendary and lightly intoxicating drink synonymous with the Pacific, was a bitter concoction made from the roots of an indigenous plant common to the islands. As a white person in a Pacific culture, I got hung up on whether or not I was going to get sick from sharing the same cup as everybody else. I took a mouthful of the rather vile drink from a coconut shell in politeness, the Kava looking more like dish water than the exotic, traditional, culturally important relaxant it was supposed to be. With the shell passed around a few times, all I felt was the placebo effect of the pending food poisoning I was certain I'd get. The locals all cheered and carried on as we drank, no doubt they'd seen this a million times, but for whatever reason it was still amusing to see white people sip on their culture.

We drove around to the usual tourist spots and passed the famous Scottish writer, Robert Louis Stevenson's home. Elei remarked that Stevenson had imported all of the timbers to make his house from Canada. The vegetation of Western Samoa was dense and dramatic, intensely wet and almost cartoonish in nature. We drove to the *To Sua* ocean trench, an enormous hole in the ground surrounded by lush greenery, its intensity only compounded by the stunningly clear ocean at the bottom. The emerald green waters were only accessible by a narrow, rickety 20m ladder to a tiny platform at the base. Amazingly, not another soul was there, as Jess and I descended into the cool waters of the pool. The nearby surf echoed as the surge of the pool dragged us around. I wondered briefly if I was going to be sucked into some kind of underwater cave and spat out the other side into the ocean.

Elei's house was half finished, made from rendered brick. The entrance was bordered with bright overgrown green grass, blades as thick as fingers, the path itself mostly a mud trench after so much rainfall. By Samoan standards, the house was large and abundant, with many families still living in traditional *fales*. Elei was clearly opting for a more western approach to living, his house having walls and furniture, unlike a *fales* which was essentially a grass roof and a flat piece of earth to sleep on. Walking in, the house was bare, looking very much like the house of a single man who cared very little about homeliness. The living room was entirely dedicated to his son, trestle tables covered in flowers, photos and objects of his memory. I wasn't sure how to handle the size of the permanent memorial, nor the recency of his son's death, however we were soon to learn it had been two years. This was not simply some photos of his son to remember, this was quite literally an entire living room dedicated to his life. Elei could see our unease, our Western sensibilities showing through again, coming from a culture which celebrates the now and pretends that death is something we can delay by purchasing a second house or third car.

Elei's son had died from *Septicemia*, a fatal bloodstream infection brought about by unhygienic use of traditional tattooing methods - the tattoo in the Pacific is considered a transition from boy to man. Known as the *Pe'a,* the piece is an enormous and intricate artwork, covering the waist to the knees. The work is extremely painful, made using traditional handmade tools: wood, turtle shell and pieces of bone. Elei had urged and encouraged his son to take on the *Pe'a,* even though in present day Samoan society it wasn't as important or revered as it once was. My interpretation of the memorial and Elei's face as he explained was that he felt responsible for the death of his only son - an irreparable sadness emanating from his body language as we stood by the kitchen bench, covered in empty cigarette packets.

I couldn't sleep, the room we were in at Elei's house was completely bare except for a bed on the ground. There was one window which was open, a warm breeze blowing through - odd animal sounds carried in the breeze. My stomach was in incredible pain. Elei had cooked us some fish he'd caught with a net from the nearby bridge. The fish he caught were small, gutted and cooked otherwise whole on the BBQ. We didn't eat anything else, only these small fish, and I wondered whether I'd caught Ciguatera fish poisoning, a common disease found in reef fish which I'd managed to avoid after so many miles at sea.

I lay doubled over in bed alone, as Jess and Elei had decided to go bat hunting. I had no idea that this was a thing anywhere on earth, but sure enough, a handful of men turned up that night in Ford trucks carrying guns, all heading off into a moonless night to shoot bats out of the night sky. While bemused and intrigued by the spectacle of shooting bats (which to me seemed a bit like shooting fish in a barrel, because bats simply hang from the trees as easy targets), I was in so much pain I wish I'd said 'yes' to having BBQ bats for dinner instead of saying 'yes' to fish for dinner.

Jess and I were more or less getting along, the distraction of land being significantly easier to manage than our captivity on the boat. This isn't to say we didn't have some special moments, but in my heart I just couldn't see a future where I moved to Washington D.C to live with her as she pursued a career in law. The closer I got to Australia, the more I thought about what kind of life I was going to live next: it was clear at this juncture that no more sailing was on the cards, I was utterly broke (but thankfully not in debt) and exhausted by the endless traveling. I needed a break, and in my heart I knew I wanted a new challenge - perhaps something more cerebral in nature, although I knew full-well I'd return to this kind of life in one guise or another.

I'd seen my parents once in the last three years, when I flew home to renew my U.S visa and take on a little work. As Western Samoa was most likely the last place I would be stopping with an accessible airport, my parents decided to visit and meet Jess, my mum constantly calling her my fiancé, which was strange to hear on the phone even though it was technically true. They flew in and we had dinner at a restaurant with Jess, before they took a bus on the south of the island where they stayed in grass huts on the beach. We visited the next day, taking the opportunity for some luxury, spending two nights sleeping in a hut and eating as much locally made food as we could.

Constellation was in desperate need of some care and work, and I was hoping my dad would spend a day or two helping me onboard. He had spent his career as a woodwork & metalwork teacher, so he was practical by nature. I felt in a way I'd never worked on any projects with my dad as an adult, having some idea in my head about how nice it would be, just dad and I working on the boat, talking about life. I'd read a book a year earlier about a father and son who sailed a *Vertue 26,* a boat very similar to *Constellation*, around Cape Horn together. I'd envisioned doing a little trip with my dad when I got home, hoping he'd take an interest in *Constellation*.

My first father, from Germany, died of a drug overdose when I was not even a year old. My mum, originally from New Zealand, was left essentially destitute in Australia without any material possessions. My biological father lived the artistic persona - full of charisma, character and creativity, yet self-destructive, untrustworthy and broke. He took record cover photos, became too friendly with female pop-stars and unsuccessfully rode the heroin-wave of the early 1980's. After his death and without a significant social network, mum moved into an Ashram. It was here that she found support and friendship, as well as the beginning of her lifelong discipline of spiritual learning and meditation. It was also here that she met my second father, from New York, and within three weeks he had asked her to marry him, as he also took on the role of my father. I could not have asked for a better father and not a day goes past where I do not think what tremendous fortune my mum and I had. My second father treated me as his own son, and absolutely no different than the biological son he would later have with mum (my brother). Yet in my soul, there was always a sense that something was missing. I could not look to my father and see myself - there was no similarity. I could not look to him and see where my own melancholy came from, my own tendency for self-sabotage and the darker aspects of the creative persona. In essence, my life was often very much driven by a search for identity.

When I asked whether he wanted to come to help for a day or two, he acted strange and said he was '*on holiday*' and didn't want to be working. I couldn't really understand his response, feeling a deep hurt. I wanted to connect with him on this adventure and I thought to myself, '*if I had a son, and he was on a perilous journey around the world, I would do everything I could to help him.*' For months I would ruminate on this emotional setback, wondering if this was a pattern in my life with him, or whether this was a singular occurrence. Again, my expectations had caused an internal rift and dialogue - perhaps dad really did just want a break. I didn't know what was going on but it brought up a certain dimension of sadness and disappointment.

The next morning I was still sick as we drove to the airport for Jess to fly home. The airport was small and dated, looking like a single building borrowed off of the airport in Honolulu. It was dawn, the air hot, wet and smelling of aviation fuel. Elei stayed in the car as I took Jess into the airport lounge, hugging her as she cried. I said '*I will see you soon!*', yet I knew deep down it was unlikely. That was the last time I ever saw Jess.

Back working onboard *Constellation* alone, my parents were still holidaying on the south of the island and everything was quiet again. After months distracted by the lights of Honolulu, Jess, discussions on the future, hurricanes and a general underlying sense of anxiety about the future, I felt a deep calm laying in my bunk staring at the cabin roof - a surface I knew every detail of, having spent hundreds of hours over the last several years looking at. I still felt a deep disappointment with my dad that I couldn't seem to shake, as I made a long list in my notebook of the critical jobs which needed doing before my departure onto Fiji - or wherever I decided I was going to go...

In the marina I made friends with a young Irishman named Dave, who was delivering a boat singlehanded for the owner in New Zealand. When we weren't working on our boats, Dave and I hung out, the bond of singlehanded sailing and the associated self-contained kind of personality connecting us. I'd noticed the similarity amongst singlehanded sailors, being that they were always very happy to connect with people, but also equally happy to be left alone. Because of this, one always felt an ease around them as there wasn't a sense they were taking or needing something from you.

The following morning at 6am, *Constellation* rumbled. She rumbled in a kind of way which felt eerily like the tanker episode thousands of miles earlier, off the coast of California. It was obviously impossible to be on a collision course while stationary in the harbour, yet I woke up in an instant, responding almost like I had PTSD. The feeling was incredibly unusual, as I jumped out of my bunk and into the cockpit at a well practiced pace. Looking around the marina, there were the heads of almost everyone on boats looking around in bewilderment. Moments later, some people cottoned onto what was happening quicker than others, as two larger boats fired up their engines, crew starting to untie from the marina in a huge rush - it suddenly dawned on me: that rumble was the ground shaking from an earthquake. Moments after that realisation, it occurred to me that an earthquake on an island could very well mean an impending tsunami.

Feeling an earthquake through the hull of a boat,

while asleep, in the water, is one of those feelings one hopes to never experience again. Afterwards, the ensuing sense of bewilderment carried itself through the air, as if the entire town of Apia had its head out the window looking at everyone else, wondering what had just happened and what to do about it - if anything. This momentary pause of quiet was simply the slingshot pulling back, before full blown chaos. As the rubber band stretches back, there is a quietness and a hesitation during the moment of aim. I looked across at Dave as the tsunami sirens installed on poles throughout Apia turned on, and the entire town descended into madness. The two vessels were now untied and reversing out of their slips, as I looked at the water which started to form strange looking currents around the pontoon pylons, much like a ripping tide. I went down below and picked up my satellite phone and passport, turning on the phone, which soon started beeping with messages. People tracking my voyage around the world had noticed earthquake activity in the region, sending me warning messages of a quake large enough to cause a tsunami, detected 600 miles south of Western Samoa.

Still watching the two larger boats attempt to exit the harbour, I looked around trying to decide what I was going to do. Of all the natural events one could experience while sailing, the management of a tsunami was not one of the topics I'd studied up on. Storm tactics, hurricanes or a mid-ocean dismasting were subjects I at least had some knowledge on, but a tsunami? All I knew was what I'd seen in movies, which if they were to be believed, meant I was going to die by way of a huge wave at any moment. The larger boats began to struggle as the marina began to eerily drain of water, signalling that if they were struggling to exit the marina with significantly bigger engines and crew, there was virtually no chance I could do it on my own with a tiny single cylinder Diesel engine which worked intermittently at best.

The sirens blared and people ran through the streets seeking higher ground. Other boat owners grabbed what they could and quite literally headed for the hills. Dave and I continued to hang around on the marina pontoons, watching the marina drain even further, wondering what on earth was going to happen next after all that water drained back out into the harbour. While the noise of all the chaos continued, the natural surroundings themselves were at utter peace. Other than the appearance of a strong outgoing tide, it was a normal, calm and perfectly still morning on an island in the South Pacific.

I always felt vulnerable on land, or near it. Deep in the ocean I felt significantly more at ease, both with myself and my surroundings. One lived a life in sync with the environment, outside of any forms of control or other people imposing themselves upon you, loneliness was virtually unheard of. At this very moment, I wished more than anything that I was in the middle of the ocean, where a tsunami would be no more distinguishable than the passing of a wave along the hull. It tore me apart that I couldn't just leave and head out into the safety of the deep. Where I was, it was completely out of control - it was as if the ocean was preparing itself to engulf an island - like the bottomless trenches of the sea were inhaling an enormous breath before exhaling us into oblivion.

Dave and I stayed close together in a kind of odd calm. It was almost as if we were both experiencing a higher level of control in the situation, because we had spent so much time alone being self-sufficient, knowing full-well that panic gets you nowhere. With our passports in hand, we walked to the marina quay wall and sat down next to an enormous tree, which was obviously old enough to have survived its fair share of tsunamis. We watched our boats hit the bottom of the marina, all tilting in unison as their keels hit rock bottom. I'd made a decision that if I was going to lose my boat after all we had been through - after all of our struggles together - the miles, the joy, the depths, the culmination of the most incredible experiences of my life... If I was going to lose my boat after all this, I was going to watch it happen. Curiously, Dave felt exactly the same way, even though the boat he was on wasn't his - but he was responsible for it, and he was going to watch till he could watch no longer. We joked that we'd climb the tree if we saw a wave coming.

The idea of a Hollywood-wave felt so improbable. Other than the sirens and the people running, the world simply seemed too calm for a 30ft wave to appear. The police were driving up and down the main road of Apia, ferrying people to higher ground, yelling out of a megaphone. They came over to us, two young white guys sitting on the quay watching their boats, telling us we'd be arrested if we didn't seek higher ground. This threat was unexpected, however we noticed police were taking people to Aggie Grey's Hotel, which wasn't too far from the marina, and we knew we could still see our boats from the top balcony.

The hotel was mostly full of patrons, all panicked, some crying. Dave and I continued to feel a sense of detachment, a feeling I am convinced came from being alone at sea: do what you can, but come what may. It sounds morbid, but I, along with many other sailors, think about death a lot, because it's a very real thing to consider, and it's best to think about it and make a plan of action rather than live in fear. In my line of thinking, if you want to avoid something, you risk-assess and play out scenarios, not shy away from the subject because it's too big or too confronting. There is nothing more confronting at sea, alone, in a small boat, than the ocean itself. So, if you are confronted every moment of the day with something larger than yourself, you see your smallness in it all, which provides clarity. I never wore a life jacket on large ocean passages, instead remaining nimble around the deck, strapping myself in only when in the cockpit for long hours on the tiller, in case I fell asleep and was thrown overboard. The reason for not wearing a lifejacket was not because I was foolhardy, but because if I was washed overboard, I wanted to die as soon as possible. The idea of floating around for days in a lifejacket, knowing full-well your boat had sailed off under windvane without you, seemed at least a thousand times worse than simply drowning as fast as possible. It was this kind of thinking that predominated as I looked out over the bay of Apia, when the water finally started to come back in.

Eight times, the marina filled - eight times the marina drained. There were no waves larger than a few feet, no Hollywood style terrors flattening the hotel we watched from. The sirens continued, the streets now lay bare, the Police and fear had done their job. Throughout all this I'd wondered how my parents were, but for some reason never considered that perhaps things could be worse on the south part of the island.

Within hours, stories started filtering through (phone towers and communications were all down) that the south of the island had actually been decimated. It was unclear what the outcome of the tsunami was, but it was now clear as the bay began to calm, the bay slowing its tidal motions and returning to normal. However, I was soon to learn that this was not the case where my parents were - the south of the island had experienced something *very* different. With this news, I ran in a panic like everyone else had just an hour before, looking for Elei to drive me to the south of the island.

Running up and down the streets of Apia, every taxi was taken as locals found rides to check on their own families in other regions of the island. I eventually found him and he said he could take me for $50. I was a bit taken aback - he knew full-well by this stage that dozens of people had died, resorts and beaches completely flattened. Without hesitation, I said I'd pay whatever he wanted to take me down, as we drove through the lush, green hills of inland Samoa. Elei wanted to talk however I couldn't muster any words, the stress of not knowing what had happened to my parents was too great, as I stared out the window, feeling somehow responsible.

Driving down the dirt road to the beach huts, the damage began to be clear - as far as one could see in either direction and 100-200 metres inland, everything was completely flattened. A powerful wave had rolled in, picking everything up in its wake and scattering it in a long line - much like the high tide line on a beach full of seaweed. Except, in this case, the line of debris consisted of cars, entire house roofs, toys, plastic rubbish and blankets covering bodies.

We drove past the tsunami line and into the beach resort, the signs all around us were obvious the shacks my parents were staying in had been lost. The question now was where are my parents and are they even alive? A young girl ran up to the taxi - I asked in a panic where everyone was, the remains of the resort were deserted. She pointed up the hill to a church, saying everyone from the resort was at the church.

My parents appeared disheveled, stressed and shaken. The wave had reached right up over the reef and barrelled right through the straw beach huts. Dad had gone for a walk along the beach at sunrise, feeling only a light tremor as he walked. He kept walking without thinking much about it, as he caught something unusual out of the corner of his eye. Looking up from the sand, he saw the wave of the tsunami hit the outer reef and explode, unlike any of the other waves he'd seen in the last week of being in the huts. Still not putting two-and-two together, he stood on the beach and watched, the water rising like a sudden tide at his feet. Before he could turn to run or even understand what was happening, a torrent of water picked him up, washing him up into the jungle. Completely submerged, he bear-hugged a tree as the water drained. Miraculously, he received only cuts and bruises to his body while a second wave thundered in, thankfully with significantly less power than the first, as he ran up further onto higher land, looking for my mum.

Mum had woken up with the tremor, going to the toilet behind the huts. As she walked around the path, she looked out to sea and saw the exploding wave, which moments later appeared on the shore, as a huge rush of water began climbing its way up towards her, flattening the hut she had just woken from. Now running, she leaped onto a concrete water tank, the water rushing and swirling around her. Standing on the tank and watching in utter shock, the water receded, causing more damage on the way out as dad ran through the wet, debris filled jungle towards her.

Astonishingly, no one at the resort or anyone from the family who ran it were injured. Soon, the sirens sounded, their delay ten minutes after the entire event. The locals knew it was possible for earthquakes to happen in quick succession, as everyone hurried to get what belongings they could find and seek higher ground, the church being the default meeting place.

Elei drove us back to Apia, my dad coming across as being much more severely disoriented and confused than mum. The airlines began bringing in more planes to evacuate tourists from the island, with Aggie Grey's Hotel somehow managing to find a room for my parents as they waited for the airline to re-route planes from New Zealand. The following morning at 2am, my parents left, flying home to Australia and appearing on the news not long after, talking about the ordeal and their narrow escape.

Many sailing boats left Samoa in the coming days, not wishing to risk another tsunami. Dave left the day it all happened which I was disappointed about - it wasn't often I came across such a like minded soul, barely getting an opportunity to say goodbye to him as he sailed off en route to New Zealand for his delivery, leaving no contact details or even a last name.

Staying on in Apia, I enlisted with the Red Cross to help in the cleanup efforts, working from a large tip truck tray, refuelling each morning before heading off into the south of the island to clean up debris, help families and hand out food. The entire Tongan navy, consisting of less than a handful of ships, were deployed with supplies, as well as helicopters to mass dump deodorants across the affected areas. One never considers the intense odour of the sea regurgitating itself onto the shores. Fish, rubbish, bodies and seaweed from the deep, all decomposing in the sun to create an environment which is almost unbearable to work in. The stories I heard from locals I worked with in the truck were devastating. We drove into small towns where the beaches were littered in bodies covered in towels, family members simply milling around, unable to completely comprehend their sudden losses. Cars were wrapped up in trees, a beach I had been swimming on two days earlier was completely unrecognisable. Each night I would go home to *Constellation*, Jess already home in the U.S, my parents back in Australia, my sailing friends already long gone, and I began to feel the need to leave.

I had a strong sense of needing to do something. I often felt my life was so selfish, just sailing around, exploring and experiencing without giving anything tangible back. It was as if I carried a constant sense of guilt, a kind of syndrome where I couldn't believe I deserved any of this, so I would somehow manage to sabotage it. The tsunami, or rather, the entire Pacific Ocean had taught me so many things, with so many near-misses. There was so much poverty in the Pacific islands, so much lost culture and heritage, so much of the West impinging their religions, their food, their rubbish, their ways... They were all here in Samoa, the signs of colonialism were obvious at every juncture. I began to feel like I was a missionary - these people didn't really need my help, I seemed to want to help not because I connected with these people or knew them, but out of some kind of strange guilt, as if to undo my selfish life, or to make up for all the damage that had been done to these islands by white people arriving on boats. In a way, people just like me. The self-loathing I felt after this enormous event was immense.

After four days with the Red Cross, it became apparent that my helping wasn't actually that useful. There was an abundance of volunteers and as often happens with these kinds of events, there are a lot of willing hands but not a lot of leadership to utilise them all. I'd heard through a handful of the last remaining sailing boats in the marina that a nearby island named Niuatoputapu had also been affected, but was significantly more isolated and in need of genuine assistance. Niuatoputapu (or 'new potato', as termed by Australians, of course) received a monthly barge delivery of food and materials, however the barge was not due for arrival for another two weeks. As such, they were low on provisions and in desperate need of the very basics we take for granted: sandals, lava lava's (shoal like material used by both men and women as clothing), galvanised nails, tarpaulins, crackers, rice, etc. Through my website, I raised a few hundred dollars from readers and bought as much as my little boat could carry from things I bought and collected around Apia.

With little fanfare, saying goodbye to Elei and some sailing friends, I departed Apia at 11am on a genuine mission with a sense of direct purpose. I rounded the island of Upon and sailed through the Apolima strait as the sun set, slowly drifting south until the water glassed over and an enormous harvest moon rose over Western Samoa, the smell of visible woodsmoke curling across the deck. The islands always seemed to have a fire burning, either for cooking, burning rubbish or clearing.

Today was more intense, with so much tsunamis debris being burned off. Diesel stacks from the enormous generators which provided electricity for the island belched diesel soot amongst the fire smoke, creating a stunningly beautiful purple haze of manmade pollution. Again at sea, this time alone for the first time in a while, I lit up my strobe light and tri-light to notify every other vessel in the vicinity I existed, and went to sleep, waiting for wind. Just an hour later, the British ensign on *Constellation's* backstay started gently flapping in the breeze, making enough sound to wake me up. I trimmed the sails and we took off towards New Potato.

After an idyllic and gentle re-entry into offshore sailing, we arrived at a reasonable hour after a textbook sail, in time for a change in the early morning with full visibility, which was a mandatory requirement for this channel entry. I praised my lucky stars after noticing things were not lining up on my chart, seeing it was clear the chart-derived GPS positions were off by 50-100 metres. I spun around and headed back out to sea, radioing another sailing boat at anchor for assistance. With a little backwards and forwards, I was eventually able to line up a set of range markers on shore. These markers provided two arrows on top of each other, which when lined up from the ocean and kept in alignment, provide safe passage through the blasted reef.

As I anchored, I looked out from the bow at a devastating scene. My dinghy was literally on its last legs, to the point where you began to sink as you rowed.

Another sailing couple came over with a motorised dinghy and took me ashore where I walked along a road of utter destruction. Families were crouched under army tents provided by the Tongan navy, who had sent one of their decrepit ex-Australian navy ships currently tied to the dock, looking like it had last been serviced during the Vietnam war. Pigs ran around alongside undernourished dogs, open black water pits and small children. It was a moment where I just stood there, detached, unable to really comprehend it all. The place was literally a war scene, the tsunami obviously decimating the island. It was also quite clear these people were still mostly living a subsistence life here, more in tune with their cultural heritage than Apia and its surrounds. A feeling of deep sadness ran through me, mixed with guilt and shame - an immense feeling of selfishness, as if peering at a spectacle from the comfort of my own lounge room. While I was there, amongst it - feeling it - I knew I could leave at any moment and continue on with my privileged life. An act these people could not perform - this was their life and they had nowhere to go because this was their everything. It always seemed as though the most impoverished - the worst off - always got the bitter end and then some.

The books of Conrad, Robert Louis Stevenson, of Bernard Moitessier, romanced these islands and I believed every word. The reality was, these were tiny third world countries, impoverished by those who thought they knew better. People who thought they knew a better God, a better life, a better way. As I walked, I couldn't understand my own presence, even though I had come here with genuinely altruistic intentions (to bring what supplies I could afford and physically carry). I had never felt so out of place, so aware of who I was and my privilege, an existence granted to me through pure luck. I had felt these feelings many times before, but they were hard to articulate and quickly forgotten by distraction. Yet here, there was no distraction, the world had presented itself to me wholly in all it's brutality.

I woke up the following morning to Christian gospel songs. Bellowing from the nearby church, the voices traveled quite a distance by the morning sea breeze. I could just make out the pews from *Constellation's* bow, strewn and mangled across the front lawn. The service still ran, everyone standing or sitting on the floor of the concrete church, singing as if their lives depended on it. It was stunningly beautiful both in sight and sound. At the same time my heart sank - what kind of God does this - what kind of God will answer the prayers of some; ignore those of others and drown small children in mud, garbage and seaweed?

Unloading what I had for these people into the cockpit looked like a pittance. I felt ashamed, what I had could barely help just one family and there were so many that needed help. I sat in my cockpit and cried, this last six months had just been so intense - the reality of nearly losing my parents just days before crashing down on me. Brynne, a half Canadian, half Samoan woman I met at the Red Cross in Samoa came alongside in a dinghy to help unload what I had. The bigger sailing boats who had larger budgets and capacity also brought what they could, as we stacked it all onto the dock. My heart lifted as I began to realise that as a combined effort, we had actually brought a lot of assistance. Singularly we brought little, but together we had enough to make a difference.

Brynne organised with the local community for us to hand out everything we had at a local hall, which had no roof. The roof was about 150 meters away, half submerged in the water - the tsunami somehow managed to dislodge the roof but leave the walls intact. Men would come by and grab a handful of galvanised nails, women and children would take rubber sandals and lava lava's. When everything was distributed, the sun was low on the horizon and I walked back along the main road. Dust and smoke in the atmosphere created beautiful lines of light in the sun. I stood behind the shadow of a coconut tree and photographed a cement water tank, which had drifted down the street, an upturned car next to it. Two beautiful small children wanted their photo taken: a small girl with a bead necklace and her brother cheekily standing hiding behind her. A teenage boy was with them and I asked if I could take his photo too, with his broad shoulders and Polynesian features. Back on *Constellation*, I looked at these images: the young children still carried a beautiful innocence in their sparkling eyes, the teenage boy already showing signs of the weight the world imposed upon him. I cannot imagine it was easy growing up here on six square miles of volcanic island in the middle of the ocean. The following morning at dawn, I drank coffee in the cockpit overlooking the large, cone shaped island of *Tafahi*, mostly consisting of the mountain it supported named *Piu-'o-Tafahi*, towering 560m above sea level. The locals told me this island grew the best Kava root in the entire Pacific, which I could believe, it's lush green surface reflecting in perfect symmetry on the glassy dawn sea. A myth speculates that Robert Louis Stevenson found the treasure of Lima, the true source of his wealth, on the island of *Tafahi* - a myth I enjoyed playing through in my head over coffee as a distraction from the shoreside carnage.

TONGA & THE FINAL LEG

As the breeze filled in, I raised *Constellation's* sails, weighed anchor and motored out of the reef pass of *New Potato*, waving to fellow yachtsmen eating lunch on deck. The voyage to Vava'u, Tonga was wet and blustery. My patience for these conditions had waned, the intensity of the previous weeks continued to put questions and doubts in my mind about the point of it all. Not just the point of sailing, but this thinking took me into a darker place where I questioned what the point of anything at all was. The passage to Tonga wasn't long enough to provide the sea miles I needed - the miles I needed to reconnect with the ocean and find some solace, peace and solitude in nature. Once again, it was the torment and turmoil of land which was affecting me so deeply - in hindsight I shouldn't have opted for Vava'u, perhaps aiming for an island further away to provide the time at sea I really needed. At the same time, Australia was looking so close on my chart, there was another great internal conflict as the realisation that it was all coming to an end continued to play on my mind. On the one hand I wanted to finish and move onto other things, but on the other hand I was terrified of what I might push myself into without a break to truly contemplate my next move.

Jess would still regularly be in contact with me, this idea that I would finish the trip and move to the U.S.A still on the cards. I knew in my heart by this stage there was no chance this would happen. After years of pushing and living like this, how on earth could I even consider moving to an apartment in Washington D.C, while my fiancé, (or wife!) went to work every morning and I invented some pointless task to undertake (a job, for example), in order to bide my time? Our messages became more strained, as I avoided turning on my satellite phone knowing full well there would be more false promises to make, more plans being made which would never eventuate. I didn't have the gumption, mental space or energy to be honest about how I was feeling - in part because I also felt so terribly confused: when Jess was around, there did seem to be a possibility for a bright future - yet when I was alone, I could not see it. Was this simply the anguish of the previous months' events? The emotion of my voyaging life coming to an end? I simply didn't know. I simply couldn't think straight.

On the chart, the island of Vava'u was made up of a cluster of small islands or passages of water weaving between interconnected landmass. It looked beautiful, a fitting last stop before Australia. By this point, I was so broke, both financially and mentally, I had no interest in exploring any more islands. Fiji was en route, along with Lord Howe Island and others, yet my desire for exploration had waned, as if thrown overboard with the dishwater or washed back out to sea with the tsunami.

It was only two days sail to Vava'u, yet the squalls were incessant, as lines of dark cloud would become visible on the horizon, quickly making their way directly for us. The sea already had a swift chop, the trade winds blowing with a strong consistency which was great for making miles, but not so great from the perspective of comfort. *Constellation* was not a comfortable boat; she was so small and bobbed like a cork, a trade swell treated her like a rag doll. While uncomfortable, she was always manageable, reliable and my greatest love. To have a love affair with an inanimate object is a curious undertaking, however I think it suited us both rather nicely. As the squalls passed by, I would reef the mainsail, furl the jib and sit in the cockpit in torrential rain. The softness of the rain was always a surprise, the harsh sun and hard salt water became the norm - yet with these little tropical surprises I was reminded that grace exists in the world, even though the wind speed doubled and the sea state whitened in a brief fury.

Vava'u began to appear on the horizon, rising 204 metres above sea level. My relief of seeing land was significantly greater than normal, the previous 24 hours of sailing being some of the most intense of the whole trip. I had spent twelve hours hove-to with 40kt sustained winds, the sea covered in spindrift. What started out as squalls turned into a full-blown and sustained storm, the winds directly on my nose.

The harbour was a well known refuge for yachtsmen, so I expected there to be a large contingent of sailors here. Closing in on the island, the wind backed off as I worked under engine through the beautiful passage into the capital of *Neiafu*, my biggest hope by this stage being that they had a nice cafe I could have a quiet dinner at. Rounding the passage into the main anchorage, it was clear why this was a yachting Mecca. The protection the islands afforded created an idyllic scene, the shore lined with small shops, an anchorage full of moorings. After the tumultuous seas of the past few days, the calmness was almost incomprehensible. *Constellation* motored through the still water, barely moving, and I wobbled about with sea legs which had become used to a significantly different rhythm.

It was too late to go ashore, instead I had an argument with Jess over Skype via the WIFI signal I was able to receive from the shore. The following morning I moved off the mooring and tied up at the commercial dock to proceed with the usual check in requirements - yet again, small islands showing their greatest capacity for burgeoning paperwork. The customs officer had a great book, full of horizontal and vertical lines, ruled by hand with every visiting boat logged in fine handwriting. After this impeccably detailed recording of my arrival, I moved off the concrete dock and back onto the mooring, before rowing ashore in my ever-sinking-dinghy. By this point, the dinghy was a joke, being over 25 years old and made of a hypalon fabric I couldn't find repair materials for. It was quite surprising we'd made it this far, the liferaft being of a similar vintage - a fun fact I thought of every time I began rowing in the dinghy, sinking one row stroke at a time. Onshore I made a beeline to the Aquarium cafe, a place I'd read all sailors frequented, because I knew it would afford familiarity, good Internet and the possibility of decent coffee.

Via my website, I'd continue to receive positive emails, messages and the occasional donation, readers often sending me anywhere from $5 to, on the very rare occasion, a lot more. The notes along with these donations was always '*I hope you can find something nice to eat!*' or, in one way or another, remarks on how they wished they had done what I was doing. The generosity was unexpected and kind, as well as something which had both gotten me out of a tight spot financially, but also emotionally. At every port with Internet, I would spend my time replying to people's emails, often full of questions, more often than not from young men my age who were looking for tips or answers on how they could sail off over the horizon. With patience I'd spend the time to reply to everyone, taking their questions and interest seriously. More often than not I never heard from them again, but every once in a while, I'd receive an email a month, or even a year, later expressing their gratitude for the reply and motivation for a trip they had undertaken. Throughout the voyage I had struggled with the apparent selfishness of my undertaking. Yet, time and time again, I found that by living my life as fully as I could - by taking risks and expressing myself in a humble way, my actions were truly inspirational to others. It began to dawn on me that it was *okay* to live my life the way I saw fit and I didn't have to carry around a perpetual guilt for being me. On more than a handful of occasions, I would bring this up with people who had helped me, being regularly surprised by their responses. They had received as much joy in helping me achieve my dreams as I had gratitude for receiving the support.

Vava'u was more established and set up for western visitors than any of the other places I'd visited since Hawaii. Many of the businesses were owned by white expats from New Zealand and Australia, the laws for business ownership in the Kingdom of Tonga being different than elsewhere. As such, the shops, cafes and restaurants had a western sensibility, the capital of Neiafu being a global hotspot for whale watching tourism. Genuine Tongan culture could be found inland, or hidden away around the fjord-like islands where families would serve Tongan feasts on the beach.

The mooring field was full of characters all anchored for varying reasons, many becoming stuck and unable to leave - through lack of funds, lack of will, a fed up wife or the breakdown of friends and crew. Certain places in the Pacific were sink-holes for dreamers, much like marinas I'd sailed through in Europe and the U.S. Boats were magnets for odd people. My friend Rob, in Sausalito, would say *'boats are bug lights for weirdos'*, the both of us knowing we were just as weird as the next.

A small 27ft yacht on the mooring next to mine, had been sailed into Tonga and gifted to the nearest person on the same day, the owner unable to spend another second on the water - the boat was now chartered to backpackers by a local cafe owner. A nearby rib restaurant was owned and run by two married couples, who had sailed in and had virtually no money left - they decided to open the restaurant as a means to keep living their dream and make some extra money. With abundant access to pigs, the idea seemed like a good one. Yet, days after my arrival, the couple were fist fighting on the street, the poor local Tongan on pork rotation duty, now breaking up a physical argument on the front lawn.

There was sometimes something slightly embarrassing about the people these remote places attracted - rabid individualists who usually didn't fit in elsewhere - the kind of people who would probably have a bunker if they owned a home. While rabid individualists were my tribe, there was an added level of dysfunction to many who sought independence in these remote outposts. Every expat seemed to have some crazy story about where they came from - often ex-military or ex-small business owners and people who simply just didn't fit anywhere else. This created a melting pot of unique and independent personalities, stuck or moving very slowly through paradise. Before long I knew it was time for me to begin my final preparations for home. This was the last leg, Tonga to Australia, and I prepared my final shopping in Neiafu.

When a sailor says they are departing the next day, virtually no one believes them. There is always a blocker which delays a departure by days, weeks, or more often than not, years. A boat not too far down from me had lost its mast and a homemade palm leaf roof was now covering the entirety of the ship. The owner lived onboard, having been on the hunt for a new mast for years. Elsewhere old men lived on boats with so much barnacle growth on their underside that it was clear they'd sailed in triumphantly, gotten used to the good WiFi, and were now unable to leave for various reasons, practical and mental. Boats have a tendency to deteriorate at an incredible rate without regular sailing, the decks piling up with junk collected by other sailors passing by: hand crank washing machines, extra jerry cans, a spare boom for when they 'finally pull up and leave', and an anchor some poor deck crew accidentally dropped over the side on departure, collected from the seabed the next day and added to the pile of liveaboard deck-junk... All this added weight pushing boats well below their intended waterline.

The islands inside Vava'u afforded weeks, maybe months of exploration for most. The crystal clear azure waters, lush greenery and ever present trade wind clouds, almost comical in appearance, dotting the horizon. I stocked up with as much rubbish food as I could carry, sourced from the general store. More ramen, rice, eggs, onions, spare water, random packets of unknown foods from China, popcorn and cans of beef stew. My intention was to sail off amongst the islands for a few days to regain my solitude and mentally prepare for the long voyage to Australia, which could take up to a month, nonstop. With little fanfare, I said goodbye to my newly found friends, a motley crew of characters, several of them were similar to my age, which was unusual. Sailing in the trade wind belt attracts a culture similar to the grey nomad crowd, usually found in RV's, caravans and old buses on land. The cost of entry into sailing usually limits the young, so it was always a pleasure to meet people my own age taking risks in small boats to see the world.

A young couple named Rob & Sarah had flown in from the U.S, renting the 27ft backpacker boat for a month. The longer story of the boat was that the owner arrived in Tonga, declaring he had been driven mad by the sea. He called his wealthy father to buy him a ticket home to Europe the same day and was never heard from again. The little boat was well equipped and I bumped into them not long after I sailed out of Neiafu, peacefully laying at anchor listening to Bob Dylan. They were as intrigued by me as I was by them and they invited me over for a drink.

For the following two days, we hung out, drinking local rum, spearfishing and talking. For a moment I felt disappointment, thinking it was more of this kind of life I had been seeking - living off the anchor in remote, beautiful places, spearfishing and talking with friends new and old who I connected with. The voyage had suddenly felt like it was always go-go-go, or taken up by visiting capitals rather than going to the more remote places I could have visited. In considering this, it became obvious I gravitated towards visiting towns because ultimately I was lonely on land and I was seeking a way to resolve that. The idea with Jess was to be able to come to places exactly like this, to be able to explore, share and discover together... The plain fact was I was thinking too much, instead of enjoying the moment - always in a state of perpetual disappointment. This thinking was compounded by the fact I was looking down the barrel of a gun, Australia just a month away, and things with Jess becoming worse as I avoided checking my email.

This overthinking and over-analysing was enough to drive anyone crazy. I knew in my heart I needed to get back out to sea where things were less confusing - where it was just myself, the elements and my shelf of great books. This didn't make weighing anchor any easier. The anchor felt heavier than it had ever been before as I disconnected *Constellation* from solid ground for the last time before my destination. Australia - the place I'd been aiming for after all these years.

Within the first 24 hours of sailing, my worries and anxiety dissolved into the sea ahead as the wind changed direction, causing me to beat into a light south west wind for a few days. Frankly I didn't care, I was simply overjoyed at finally having broken my negative spell, letting go of everything and submitting myself to whatever might come. The temperature at these latitudes began to drop quickly, the first obvious sign we were slowing exiting the South Pacific. My ability to think straight in hot conditions was poor, which had affected the amount of reading I'd been able to achieve. With the cooler climate came a reading renaissance in my bunk, a welcome change from simply trimming sails, eating cans of stew and ruminating.

Looking at my chart, it was with great joy I noticed we had found ourselves on the exact opposite side of the world to England. We'd sailed so far west of Greenwich, we were now east of it. I remembered some years before, crossing zero degrees longitude with Johannes Erdmann as we attempted to sail to Hamburg, which now felt like a lifetime ago. I watched in wonderment as the GPS slowly ticked over to 180 degrees 0 minutes 0 seconds. In a flash it was over, and the seconds of longitude began to decrease and the units started the countdown back to zero degrees. I contemplated the fact that these imaginary lines criss-crossing the globe, made up by mathematicians during the golden age of sail, were still collectively in use today, for no other reason than because all seafarers decided they existed.

I made the terrible mistake of reading a book by the food critic Ruth Reichl: Lobster risotto, latte cotto, a light lemon custard served with marinated berries... It was torturous. With further reading I reached a chapter on a Japanese sushi restaurant, deciding I should perhaps go fishing. Rob and Sarah were avid fishermen, gifting me a new set of lures for my voyage home. I hadn't had much luck in the Pacific, but my knowledge of fishing doubled from nothing to something after Vava'u, so I decided to give it a proper go.

Listening to music in my bunk and simply staring at the companionway, I heard the line spinning as I jumped out into the cockpit to catch the 400 pound line with my bare hands and cleat it, watching in wonderment as the largest Mahi I've ever seen jumped into the sky. I was attempting to catch Sashimi for one, but instead, I caught enough for an entire restaurant. *Constellation* literally slowed down under the power of the fish. Somewhat terrified, I rolled in the Genoa to make battle.

With the fish swimming under full thrust in the opposite direction, I couldn't hold it, even after putting on a pair of gloves. Deciding in the end to let it tire, I watched with a sense of sadness as it thrashed about, slowly becoming slower in its movements. While the initial thrill of catching the fish subsided, all I could think about was that this was tantamount to killing an entire cow for a single steak. Because I had no refrigeration, I could really only eat it fresh - the rest would go to waste. My decision was to reel it in and release, however as I got it closer to the boat, the fish suddenly sounded, the line whizzing out of my hands as it dove to the bottom like a harpooned whale. Soon, the line went slack again as I began to reel back in, eventually the Mahi popped up on the other side of the boat, the line now wrapped under the keel. The giant Mahi gave one last thrust of power, perhaps its last push of energy before giving up, breaking the line or the knot as it swam to freedom, a large pink lure most likely stuck in its mouth. Once again, I decided fishing was not for me, retiring to my bunk with a book on Alexander Von Humboldt: "... *Yet what we feel when we begin our long-distance voyage is nonetheless accompanied by a deep emotion, unlike any we may have felt in our youth. Separated from objects of our dearest affections, and entering into a new life, we are forced to fall back on ourselves, and feel more isolated than we have ever felt before.*" It was not the first time I had fished over all these miles, but it was my last.

On the website chronicling my voyage, there was a small form through which people could message me, sending a text to my satellite phone wherever I was in the world. Each morning I'd turn the phone on in anticipation, receiving little jokes, good wishes and tips from friends and strangers. I specifically had a note on the website asking people *not* to send me weather information, having in the past had random people send me storm notifications for areas I was not even in, creating a sense of anxiety rather than assistance. Someone messaged, mentioning that Jessica Watson, the young girl attempting to take the youngest solo circumnavigation record from fellow Australian Jesse Martin, was supposedly in the vicinity of my track. I spent the day on deck, simply looking out to sea for any sign of a little mast, a young girl on a tremendous adventure which far surpassed the grit of mine.

The leg thus far had been quite idyllic, perhaps some of the best sailing of the entire voyage. The sea lay relatively flat with a minimal swell, a light 10-15kt breeze on the starboard quarter. This kind of sailing is what I'd imagined the entire Pacific to be, the name itself derived from *Pacifico*, translating to *Peaceful*. Whomever came up with the name had clearly only sailed in this small portion of the world's largest ocean, because for thousands of miles I had experienced very little *peace*!

As I passed 160 miles south of New Caledonia, the signs in the sky were unusual and grey. More often than not, the weather was stable, interrupted only by squalls which lasted at best an hour or two. However, every once in a while, a proper low pressure system arose - the tell tale signs now above my head.

The sea began to build and build, and before long spindrift began to appear - foam terrifyingly streaked across the surface of the water. It was always at this point that I began to feel a little sick - not seasick, just sick in the knowledge that life was about to become *very* uncomfortable. The physique of the ocean surface changes in shape to a harder chine, the water creating a louder *slap* upon the hull with each crest. *Constellation* was shipping green water over the deck, our progress slowing. By early evening, we lay hove-to as I listened to the crashing water and watched the rising and falling swell through the companionway in my bunk.

Sleep was hard to find as there were so many unusual and new sounds in these conditions. A cross swell created unexpected reverberations, the stress on the boat creating new creaks I hadn't heard before. In a half-dream-half-sleep state, I woke to the immense sound of a hard breaking wave upon the hull. I remembered that out of every 10 waves, one was twice the size of the other 9. The crash was so immense, the boat shuddered, throwing objects across the cabin which had never been dislodged throughout the entire voyage. Immediately after the impact, there was a loud hissing sound from forward of my bunk. Were we about to sink?

With a surprising amount of calm, I heaved out of bed to assess with my feet how much water was entering the boat. Surprised there was no water as yet, I made a mental checklist of everything I needed to abandon - first, the grab bag, containing offshore flares, flare gun, EPIRB and some chocolate... Actually no, wait, there is no chocolate because I ate it one day in a fit of despair... Next - my life jacket, making a quick mental note not to forget my survival suit that Paul gave me in Amsterdam. Let's be frank, the chances of my 20 year old life raft actually working were slim: an image of myself in an orange suit trying to fire wet flares came to mind. This was all happening in milliseconds as I reached for my headlamp, shining it throughout the cabin in search of the hole or signs of damage. To my incredible amusement and relief, there was no damage or water pouring through the hull. The hissing had come from the triggering of my automatic inflating life jacket, which had had its release cord caught on the wet locker clothes hook, springing to life when the boat was hit by a rogue wave.

Each day was another day closer to Australia. Each day I thought about what was next, starting to relish every moment in the knowledge that it would soon be over. Each day I spent hours in the cockpit, or my bunk, simply staring out to sea or at the various trinkets around my boat as they wobbled around with the boat's motion. I pondered whether it was worth it, all this pushing to get here, the coastline well within reach on my chart.

Yes. It was worth it. Every moment, every second, every terror, every disappointment, every joy, every wave, every squall, every tear. There were so many things I would miss, but there were also many I would not. I would miss all the minute details of a solitary existence - the sounds, the solitude, the power in being fully in control of one's destiny (within the confines of nature), the daily beauty and changing ocean, which gifted me a different experience every second of the day and night. I probably wouldn't miss the food. Or the financial pressure... I thought to myself, perhaps if I do this again, I might buy a slightly larger boat - conscious that *Constellation* was a beautiful friend, I was wary of saying anything negative about her, especially when there were still hundreds of miles to go.

I'd miss the joy of immersing myself in books for hours at a time. I'd miss operating completely on my own time schedule, without a care or an interruption in my own universe of my own making. The meditative staring at the sea would be greatly missed, the hours I spent on a daily basis simply looking at the changing waves, the wind, the sky, the immense nightly dome of galaxies above, stars, planets and sheer immensity. I knew deep in my heart, I'd had a profound experience with the planet. I felt that I truly understood its fragility and uniqueness. Some years later I would read about astronauts experiencing what was termed the *overview effect*, a cognitive shift in awareness when viewing the earth from above. While I didn't get to see the earth from above, I felt I got to see it with a similar, almost reversing effect, as I peered back into the night sky in a very special way, while seeing endless horizons - distinct moments of brief all-encompassing comprehension. To say these moments were spiritual would not do them justice - I could almost feel the synapses in my brain begin to bend and twist into something else, usually after several nights of good sailing or being totally becalmed - when I could take my focus away from worrying about the present and be in the immense present.

The sun rose, the sun set. I discovered a trick whereby microwave popcorn could be made in a pressure cooker. Most days became more contemplative. I would dream about what was next, or wonder why I hadn't been popping popcorn like this for the last 2.5 years.

With basic email access, I was also able to send short messages to Twitter. I sent out the message '*Constellation is for sale, email me for more information*'. Even though I hadn't made it home quite yet, I knew my bank balance was zero, and that while my life of adventure would never end, my life of adventure with *Constellation* would sadly be ending very soon. I needed to sell her to work out what I was doing next. I tried hard to be logical and emotionless about this fact, pushing back the sadness of it all. She was an inanimate object, right? Or was she? It was hard to tell after so many miles, counting 28,000 kilometres traveled together. From moments of spiritual awakening to moments of brutal reality, and now I was going to callously sell her.

Each day I would continue filming, usually using the camera as an opportunity to complain about something. I wondered what it would all look like when it was cut together and edited. I began to worry I hadn't shot enough of the beauty and insight on this voyage, thinking maybe it was full of reluctance and negativity. The camera was my crutch to lean on with no one to talk to, decompress with or to be buoyed by. The closer we got to Australia, the more I talked into the lens, trying to process everything.

At this point we were sailing towards Brisbane. I changed my mind in good conditions and began redirecting to Coffs Harbour, another port of official entry on the eastern seaboard. There were only a handful of ports along the east of Australia where you can enter from, deciding Coffs Harbour would be a fairly relaxed entry and closer to my final destination, which continued to be Melbourne (home).

The most alarming reality to how close I was to Australia came when I was flown over by a white Australian customs plane, requesting my details and destination. As they drew circles above me, I diligently answered their questions, the intrusion of their presence confounding me to the point where I forgot the phonetic alphabet. "Yes, the boat name is C-o-n-s-t-e-l-l-a-t-i-o-n, C for Car, O for... Orange, N for... nelly..." I wondered what they thought of me, in this tiny boat from England, unable to remember my phonetics... Alfa, bravo, charlie, delta, echo... I embarrassingly opened another bag of popcorn and made a pot of rice for dinner with a can of oysters and chilli sauce thrown in for good measure.

I received an email from someone firm on buying *Constellation*. They had been following my trip, knew the story and knew the boat, and the money was waiting for my arrival. This was an immense surprise, I expected the process to take months, *Constellation* being an unusual boat. I'd also secretly hoped it *would* take months, perhaps the added time might create an opportunity to keep her somehow. The new owner was a high speed trader for Deutsche Bank, the cost of *Constellation* was his Christmas bonus. On the one hand I was deeply sad that *Constellation* was going to someone who could afford what I had struggled to keep afloat for 3.5 years with just their Christmas bonus... I wasn't sure someone who hadn't struggled for every penny could appreciate this little old boat or the amount of work required to keep her going - I also knew there was a high chance that anyone who bought her and knew the story would be buying her because in some way they wished to undertake something similar. The idea that *Constellation* had proven herself to be able to cross an ocean, in a way allowed others to dream they could also do it, since the boat could. I slowly overcame the whole situation in the knowledge that I at least would have a small runway of money to start my next thing, whatever that was. The new owner also promised to take her long distance solo sailing - his dream was to sail to Lord Howe Island, among other places. I came to accept this over the coming days, with just 200 miles to go.

The conditions and water began to slowly change, the usual telltale signs of an approach to land. The sailing was gentle and I was glad our final two days would be kind sailing for both *Constellation* and I. My mind was exhausted by how fast things were now happening: *Constellation* was all but sold, I would be on land in just two days and Jess was already emailing and asking when I planned to fly to Washington D.C. It was all a bit much, really. I just wanted to stare at the wavelets some more and let all these details sink to the bottom of the ocean. Alas, this was all of my own doing and it was time to face the music. The voyage had to end, it couldn't go on forever... I also had new things I wanted to think about - I hadn't stopped thinking about this project since the moment I conceived it, at some point near the Arctic circle while in Norway, nearly four years earlier.

LAND

On the horizon I saw the friendly white sails of another sailing boat. I called them on the radio to ask about whether they knew if Customs & Quarantine ran 24 hours a day, knowing my ETA was going to potentially land me on a Saturday night - if they kept standard office hours I would be quarantined to my boat until Monday. The idea of this was horrific; to literally be sitting on the anchor for a day and a half as the destination I had fought for lay within a hundred metres. The radio crackled as the sail boat tried to understand what I was saying: "*Customs*? What do you mean, where are you coming from, over"... "*Tonga*", I replied, feeling slightly chuffed. "*Tonga*??? Please repeat, over", "*Yes, the Kingdom of Tonga, in the South Pacific*"... "*Oh*" came their reply, as I waited. With a larger mast and greater radio power, they were able to radio a shore station and relay my question. Customs knew about my pending arrival, I assume because they'd been notified by the plane a couple of days earlier. With joy, the message was relayed that they would wait for my arrival.

Constellation began to pick up the 2kt south current which ran along the coast of Australia, as I was coming in from a more northerly position, down into Coffs Harbour. On a perfect beam reach with the current, we were flying along at 7kts. *Constellation* was sailing so beautifully, her ensign flapping happily in the breeze on the backstay, my yellow quarantine flag flying in the spreaders, just above the German courtesy flag which I flew in honour of my biological father.

With land in sight, I stood on the bow and cried. The combination of joy in doing what I had set out to complete after all these years, coupled with the sadness of it all ending, broke me down. The sky was grey, the sea flat and the wind and currents continued to push me even faster into port as my tears fell onto the bow. It was as if the universe came together to give me this last lift into home.

As we approached, the immensity of it all distracted me from proper navigation. It was past Customs & Quarantine closing time, however they knew I was literally just coming in, as the Coffs Harbour ground station called me up on the radio and asked where I was going. "*Where am I going?*" I replied, somewhat confused. The volunteer said I was approaching the wrong side of the quay, as I quickly checked my charts and position - I was in fact, heading directly for the beach, rather than the break wall! I couldn't believe my stupidity. I quickly crash gybed *Constellation* around, headed back out to sea, correctly found the entry buoys and started my entrance again. I was cursing myself for being wrapped up in my own head instead of concentrating on the task at hand - I very nearly crashed into Australia, a potentially dramatic end to the voyage indeed!

We sailed into the first break wall as I wrestled the mainsail down (by this stage it had been up for 27 days). With *Constellation* motoring in circles while I prepared the boat, I couldn't help but feel the normality of it all. It was as if I'd just gone out sailing for the day and was returning.

With *Constellation* tidy, I proceeded into the main marina. I passed a few boats with people on the decks drinking wine - they noticed this tiny little boat, beaten up, a handful of sponsorship stickers along her hull, the quarantine flag in full view. Some realised I'd come from somewhere far away and clapped. There was a tear in my eye in someone recognising this moment - I had no friends or family to greet me on the dock and I arrived completely alone, without fanfare or even the face of someone I knew.

As I berthed, Customs & Quarantine came down with their guns and uniforms. "*Where is your welcome party*", the first officer remarked. I laughed, perhaps in embarrassment, or disappointment, commenting that they were it. In a sense, my arrival was very much like my official departure years back from Monnickendam, Holland, where I simply slipped the lines, said goodbye to the dock master and began a voyage which would take 2.5 years and 28,000 km to complete. What was this feeling anyway, of being disappointed no one was there to greet me? Was it my ego wanting recognition? Or did I just want to see a familiar face after all this time? It was time to stop thinking. My arrival reminded me of the inimitable Bill Tillman, the British mountaineer who took up sailing in his 50s. Tillman would undertake enormous trips through Greenland and other far away places, only to arrive home at his berth in Lymington (curiously, the town in which *Constellation* was actually built) a few months later as if nothing had happened.

Customs searched my boat, asked me a lot of questions, removed a ton of food and a few trinkets from the islands. I watched on slightly nervously, not because I had anything to hide, but because it's strange having someone go through your home with a fine tooth comb. Everything onboard seemed to either be wet or rusty, as the poor officers reached into the grotty bilges. Eventually, with a handful of yellow Quarantine rubbish bags next to the boat, the officers sat down in the cockpit for me to complete the paperwork. It was at this point I was told I needed to pay import tax on the boat within the next week. In the end, after it was all said and done, of all the countries to enter in the world, Australia was the most bureaucratic and the most painful. Being an Australian entering into one's own country made little difference, the machinations of bureaucracy had come to spear and destroy any last traces of my free spirit. It was clear as I sat in the cockpit with the officers, that the ocean was truly the last bastion of human freedom. I felt a panic and a strong anxiety well inside me, everything was screaming *"go back out there"*. I played the scenario over and over in my head: *"I'm sorry officers, but, I need to go. Yes, I need to go right now, no need for any more paperwork, let me just get some fresh water and I'll be off."* Of course this was all going on in my head as I signed box after box, before it was all done and the officers left for a nice weekend with their families in this coastal town.

By now it was 7pm on a Friday night, as I motored over to a spare slip, tying up *Constellation* and walking to the nearest pub. I stood in a rowdy line, the noise and people slightly overwhelming. Social interaction always felt awkward for the first day back amongst people, I was shy and spoke even more quietly than normal. The woman taking my order leaned over the cash register and put her hand to her ear so she could hear me. With a table number, I sat at a bench seat overlooking the harbour. Here I was, in Australia, looking back out to sea from where I had come from. A beer and burger arrived, as I tasted the first cold drink I'd had in nearly a month. There was so much anticipation for this moment, nothing could satisfy my expectation. Walking back to *Constellation* after dinner, it was dark and I was a little wobbly on my feet, not because one beer had sent me over the edge, rather that my inner-ear would take some time to re-adjust to solid earth.

My sleep aboard was restless. It was too still and there were new noises as *Constellation* rubbed against the dock. My mind began to wander into problem-solving mode, thinking about the tax and duty bill, the sale of *Constellation*, where on earth I was going to go after *Constellation* sold, since I had no other real-world possessions. After all this, was I going to move into the spare room at my parents house?

The anticlimax of it all felt palpable.

Waking up early, I watched the sun rise from the top of the nearby hill, the same sun I had watched rise hundreds of times before from the sea. This moment gave me a sense of calm, allowing myself some joy and gratitude for my accomplishment, something I rarely allowed myself to feel, being caught up in my own angst and firmly stuck inside my head. The sheer beauty of the sun as it rose up over the ocean was a stark reminder that this is what it had been truly all about. Nature had a beautiful way of pulling me out of my own inner thoughts and into a bigger reality. This was the lesson I had learned after all these miles and this is what I had sought. All the minutiae and logistics of the voyage itself were simply obstacles to finding a sense of peace within the natural environment. Walking back down the hill to *Constellation*, I had a renewed sense of energy, a new sense of purpose, and an acceptance that what I had just done wasn't meaningless.

Jack had been tracking the voyage, timing his arrival from Berlin just two days after my arrival into Coffs Harbour. These two days were spent organising a customs broker to import *Constellation* into the country and my good friend Marty who had been helping me in a myriad of ways along the entire voyage (the truth being, without his help along the way, I might not have made it at all) loaned me the money I needed for the import. In town I perused the bookstores, the woman at the counter asked how I'd achieved such a great tan! I laughed and replied that I had just spent the last six months sailing alone across the Pacific Ocean. She laughed and then realised I was serious, probing for more of the story. It was nice to have someone interested in the voyage, as I regained my ability to actually speak to people. I regaled her with the tale of my trip and my arrival the night before, much to her wonderment. That afternoon, the local newspaper knocked on *Constellation's* deck as I was down below tearing everything out of lockers to dry, the pontoon covered in wet cushions, sleeping bags, and rusty cans. The following day I was in the newspaper, the occasional person coming down to the marina specifically to see *Constellation* and hear more about my journey.

The arrival of Jack was fun. To think, years before, he had heard this mad idea and taken a risk on whether it would actually happen or not, and here he was - sitting onboard *Constellation*, in Australia, smoking a cigarette - the dream achieved. That evening we drank a little rum I still had stashed in the oily bilges and reminisced. Jack took out the video camera and asked me whether I was disappointed about my arrival. In truth, I would have loved some friends or family to have been there for me, however I had no expectation of helicopters, chase boats or media on the dock. This was a very personal, introspective voyage. While there was some media interest in magazines, radio and newspaper in other countries along the way, interest in Australia itself was nonexistent, except for the minor piece by the local paper the day before. Perhaps Jack could see a disappointment in me I was covering up, perhaps the rum would expose a desire for things which never eventuated, for an external validation of the achievement. That didn't happen, as I exclaimed on camera, "*this is reality.*"

After two days in Coffs Harbour, we boarded a train south to Sydney. *Constellation* would sit for at least a month in the marina while the details of her sale were made final. In the meantime, I needed to go home to Melbourne, get a job and make some money so I could work out my next plan. The trappings of land and the familiarity of Australia were unexpectedly nice. In Sydney we stayed with Jack's brother in a nice home, where I felt a sense of comfort for the first time in a long while. We drank coffee and ate nice food. A sparse, minimal and hard life at sea made all these small things a thousand times better. Having someone make you a coffee, sitting down and chatting with a friend. These little moments of life were amplified, my senses overwhelmed by a big city.

In Melbourne, Jack and I visited my parents, where little had changed, except for the addition of a new family dog. I couldn't put my finger on it, but something was different about my dad. He seemed to have a curious kind of forgetfulness about him or a mild confusion about things in general. Mum had taken him to see a doctor, who said he was suffering from a kind of post traumatic stress syndrome from the tsunami in Samoa. Jack interviewed my parents about my voyage. They had been supportive of my life, however they were not seafarers, nor adventurers of this kind. I think it was hard for them to truly understand the gravity of the project. I was still disappointed at my dad's disinterest in helping onboard *Constellation* in Samoa, although the reason why would soon unravel.

I spent a few weeks around Melbourne, doing bits of work and completing negotiations for *Constellation*'s sale. The new buyer wanted the boat in Sydney and I agreed to deliver her from Coffs Harbour. The buyer also had a small light plane - I guess *Constellation* was another toy to add to his fleet. I flew back to Sydney, the new owner of *Constellation* offering to fly up to Coffs Harbour in his tiny British plane with cloth wings. We drove out to a country hangar, pushed the plane out onto the runway and flew very close to the ground for a few hours until we reached the marina where *Constellation* lay. With permission from flight control, we circled over as I peered down at the beach I nearly sailed into upon my arrival. The new owner looked over the boat and finalised the paperwork.

With a good forecast of northerly winds, *Constellation* and I were back out at sea. It was a reluctant voyage, there seemed to be no joy in delivering what was now someone else's boat. I felt somewhat seasick as night fell, coastal sailing was still much more difficult than ocean sailing. The coastline was littered with large tankers, hauling coal up and out of Newcastle to ports north and south. The coal coast. Stopping in at Port Stephens, I slept quietly on a mooring amongst gum trees. This was the first time I'd had the opportunity to really sail around in my home country. I woke to dolphins, the sight of a Koala in a nearby tree and the laughter of Kookaburras. This was my last morning in the wilderness with *Constellation*, rejoicing in the perfection of how Australian this moment was.

The sail into Sydney harbour was iconic, my first time in reaching the city by water. I sailed past the Sydney Opera House, dodging the immense water traffic - ferries, yachts, water taxis, jet skis. Under full sail we reached a bridge, the timing impeccable as our arrival was in time with the scheduled opening. It felt like I was back in Holland for a brief moment, the infrastructure of the city moving and allowing us to pass.

On a mooring for a week while the transfer of funds was arranged for *Constellation*, three friends from Melbourne visited so I could take them for one last sail. They were all avid supporters of my voyage, former work colleagues who were much older than me but all took a keen interest in supporting my dreams. We sailed around, all barely fitting onboard for the trip around Sydney harbour. This would be the final sail for me aboard *Constellation*, as the new owner, his Russian wife and her two kids arrived for the handover.

With *Constellation* on a pontoon, I stood back as the small children climbed around the boat, in and out of the hatches, pulling on the sheets, playing with the winches and untying lines from cleats. It was such a difficult scene to watch after all these miles. I tried to think bigger thoughts, knowing the money was in my account and I could move on and start something new.

Clearing *Constellation* out, I filled rubbish bins at the marina with junk from the voyage. My guitar was seized, the strings corroded, I could see it poking out of the bin from my mooring. Other than bare essentials, *Constellation* was now cleared out. I left a bottle of wine for the new owner in the galley, called the marina manager on the radio for a pickup and took the bus to the airport.

With nowhere else to go, I ended up at home in the bedroom I grew up in with my parents, while I worked out where and what I was going to do. My dad continued to act strangely as my mum began to worry, taking him to see more doctors. After much confusion and intrigue on the part of the doctors in diagnosing what was wrong with him, it was eventually revealed he was suffering from Lewy body Dementia, an aggressive and fast acting form of early onset dementia. Dad was just 59. He had been hiding the symptoms. At work where he was a woodwork teacher, he had begun by not helping students take measurements, his spatial awareness being the first to begin its rapid degradation. In the end, dad couldn't help me on my boat in Samoa because he was hiding the fact he could barely work with his hands any longer. I read about the disease and its outcome and cried in my bed.

Things with Jess fell apart entirely over a Skype conversation - I wasn't moving to Washington DC - the whole engagement was premature and immature... I felt so embarrassed, but I also felt a sense of relief I suppose. I think we both knew long before the conversation that the end was nigh.

For the weeks, months and years to come, any moment without distraction would lead me back out to sea - to those moments of sitting peacefully in the cockpit of *Constellation*, watching the raw beauty of nature unfold in the present. With time I forgot the hardships, the mistakes, my own follies. What remained of my memories were the sublime and unexplainable - with each day forward, the voyage became richer, more beautiful and imbued with meaning.

The old adage that it is '*not the destination but the journey*' was in many ways true, however the intensity of the journey was such that it would take years for many lessons to actually percolate back up from the depths of their creation. In hindsight, much angst was spent in an expectation that my spiritual quest might yield immediate results. Truth be told, the role of the quest was not to yield results until the vessel were ready to handle them - lesson #1 (of many) - live in the moment and understand the spongy nature of the soul - an entity that is forever soaking in experiences, but has a tendency to wait for an ideal moment to exhume those lessons.

When will that moment grace us? Nobody knows, perhaps it won't. But the lesson is created and the work is done - we can forever live in hope the lesson is for us, and if not, take joy in knowing its existence in the universe for the next restless adventurer.

AFTERWORD

The last remaining words of this book were eventually finished in a small fortressed town in Southern France - a creative detour as part of a new adventure - the continuation of my circumnavigation started in *Constellation* all these years later: an overland expedition in a small British four-wheel drive - from Australia to Europe via Africa.

The year now is 2020. There have been many adventures of the spirit, the soul and the heart, since all those miles at sea were laid down as invisible tracks upon the Atlantic and Pacific. My dear little boat was sold on from the Deutsche Bank trader - he never did do that passage to Lord Howe island - the second owner, Andrew, inspired by my adventures, then attempted to sail to New Zealand. Unfortunately his adventure quickly came unraveled, being rescued in Bass Strait by a Japanese grain tanker, just days after departure, *Constellation* set adrift. Salvaged by fishermen, she was towed into port and sold back to Andrew for the salvage fee. Severely damaged by her time in the ocean without a captain, *Constellation* sat in a marina, rotting, for over a year.

One day while walking under construction scaffolding in Melbourne, I received a call from Andrew - he offered to sell me *Constellation* for $1 - I said yes. At the time, I had also bought another sailing boat in Sausalito, named *Harmony*. The reality was, I didn't last long amongst the non-boat owning classes - just months into the aftermath of selling *Constellation*, an Aries 32 named *Harmony* came into my life. In a curious situation, I had now ended up with *two* sailing boats - one severely damaged and the other all the way over in California. Not much had changed with my financials, my bank account ebbing and flowing between red and black, as always.

As a means to put my mind and energy into something else (and hopefully produce enough money to go sailing with *Harmony*), I started a small tech business with my friend of many years, Marty - the friend who had gotten me out of more than one difficult situation along the way. After a year of grinding in small business with Marty, I was soon in debt and broke - my only asset was *Harmony*. As it were, *Constellation* was more of a liability than an asset, however truth be told I couldn't afford either! With a heavy heart, I gifted *Constellation* away for $1, to someone who promised a full restoration - unfortunately, to this date, the restoration has not taken place.

Selling everything I had accrued over the years since my voyages with *Constellation*, I flew to California and sailed *Harmony* back to Sydney - this adventure is another story unto itself... I eventually sold her in Sydney, getting myself out debt and becoming truly boat-less after many years. I worked hard in my business, bought a house in Tasmania, and then everything came to a standstill when my dad passed away. His passing shook me. He was the second dad I had lost, and again everything in my life came into existential question.

It took some years to recover from losing him. As the months and years went by, I could feel the time was coming again to set off. Spending six weeks in France, I worked as a photographer for the 50th anniversary race of the original *Golden Globe Race* in 1968. In Les Sables d'Olonne where the race was to begin, I met Sir Robin Knox-Johnston and other small boat luminaries. I explored Moitessier's boat *Joshua*, sat in the cockpit of *Suhali*, and wandered the decks of three of the *Pen Duick* boats so famed by Eric Tabarly. Returning from France, I was re-energised, perhaps finally the funk and emotion of the last several years had lifted. I was back.

At home in Tasmania, I drank tea in my cabin - a 20ft shipping container I had converted myself, as a means to live minimally and affordably. Each night I would lay awake in my bed wondering what journeys the container had taken, how many laps of the planet it might have done.

An adventure has a tendency to take hold of you, involuntarily - like any good creative idea, they can quickly become an obsession. A fortunate person comes across many ideas, yet not all of them stick: maybe there are failed adventures, failed attempts at creating something - anything. Yet when they stick, they stick. I knew this from my sailing adventures, when an idea has the right timing and the right energy, it cannot be stopped from being expressed.

With some false starts, an adventurous idea arose. I'd sailed the Atlantic, crossed the Pacific twice and also done a bunch of other sailing - in my heart, I knew it was time for something new - it was time to see the world from a different perspective. With that, came about my dream to finish my circumnavigation I had started in *Constellation* by other means. With a twist and a nod to my adventures in Norway, the home of my first dreams with *Constellation*, my new challenge would end there: to drive from the most southern road in Australia (South East Cape, Tasmania), to the most northern road in Europe (North Cape, Norway), via Africa in an old Land Rover named Penny.

The madness continues.

ACKNOWLEDGEMENT

Thank you to Ryan Jaffe & Martin Gleeson for always being there. Thank you to Jack Rath for believing in my dream and tirelessly creating the documentary *Between Home* - we had some adventures together hey!

Thank you Lianda Burrows, for patiently editing my work and providing positive encouragement & ideas throughout the process.

Thank you to my beta readers for your kind and helpful suggestions: Rob Tryon, Ladonna Buback, Jane Turner, Niklas Schaaf, Lynda Lim, George Droumev & Chris Tanner.

Thank you to all of those who supported me on my journey - the list is long - you know who you are, and I dare not attempt to recall everyone, for fear of missing just one of you!

ABOUT THE AUTHOR

Nick Jaffe is a sailor, photographer, writer, artist and incessant traveler. When not at sea, on the road or in a plane, he lives by the ocean in remote Tasmania, Australia.

The Years Thunder By is his first book.

For more info, future projects and updates please visit www.nickjaffe.com.au

If you enjoyed this book, please leave a review wherever you purchased it (Amazon, etc).

www.ingramcontent.com/pod-product-compliance
Lightning Source LLC
Chambersburg PA
CBHW020856020526
44107CB00076B/1873